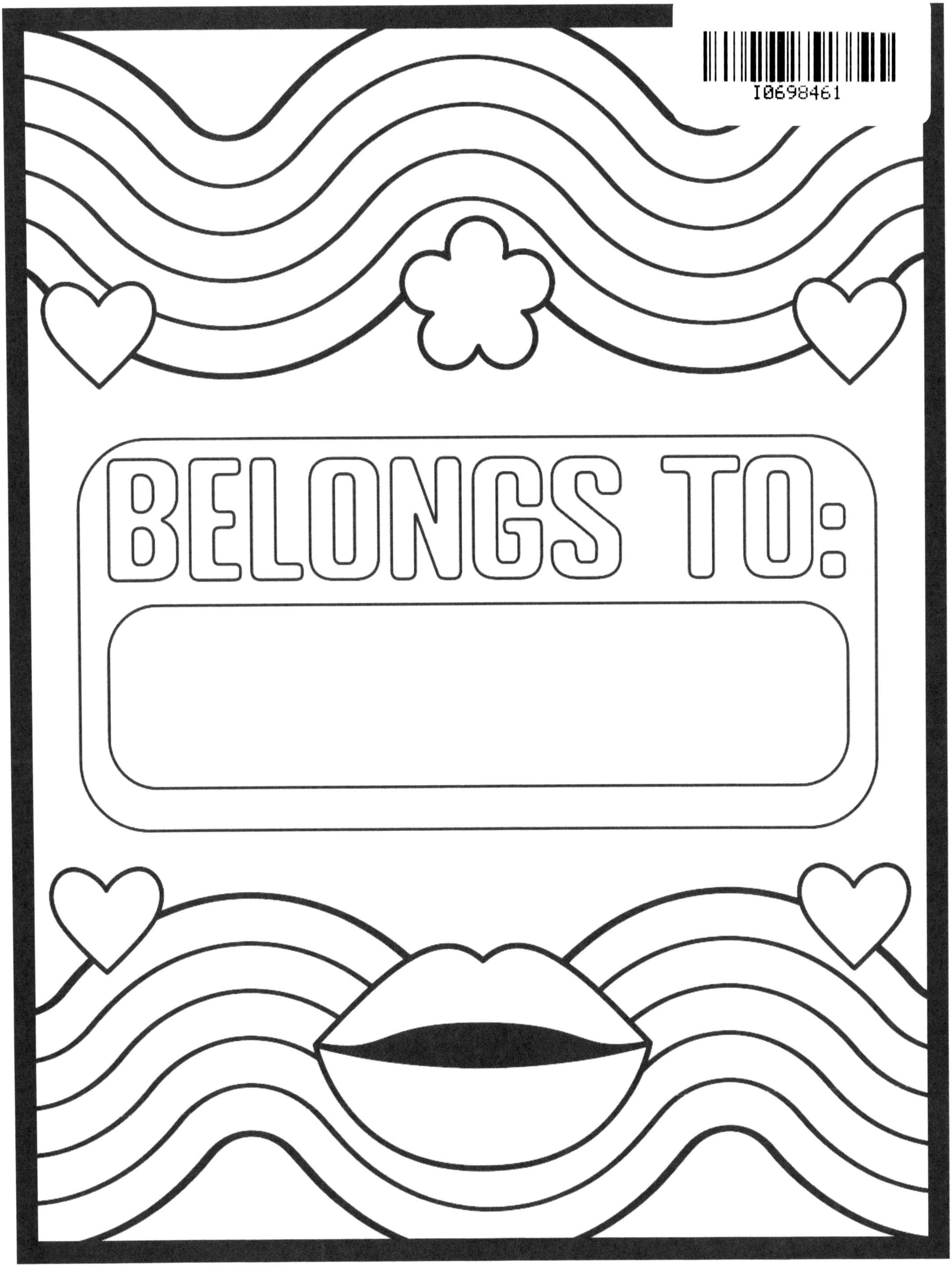

BELONGS TO:

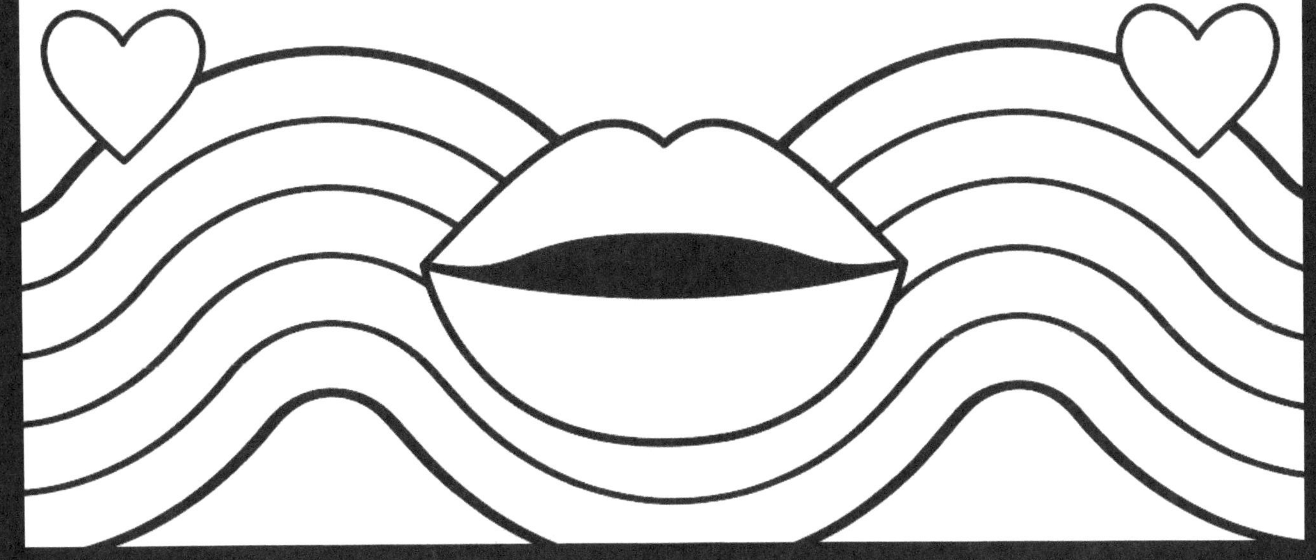

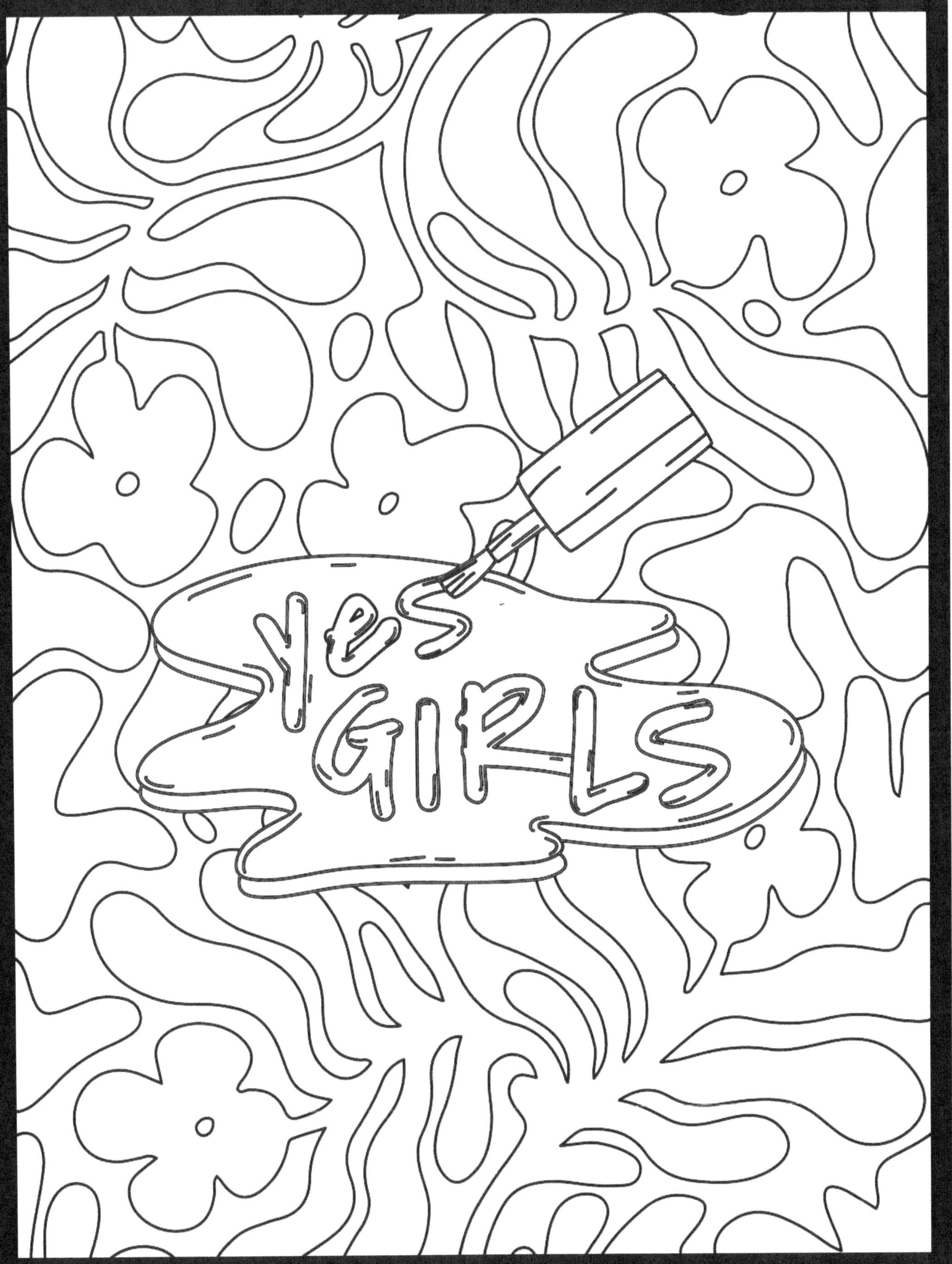

yes
GIRLS

YES GIRL!

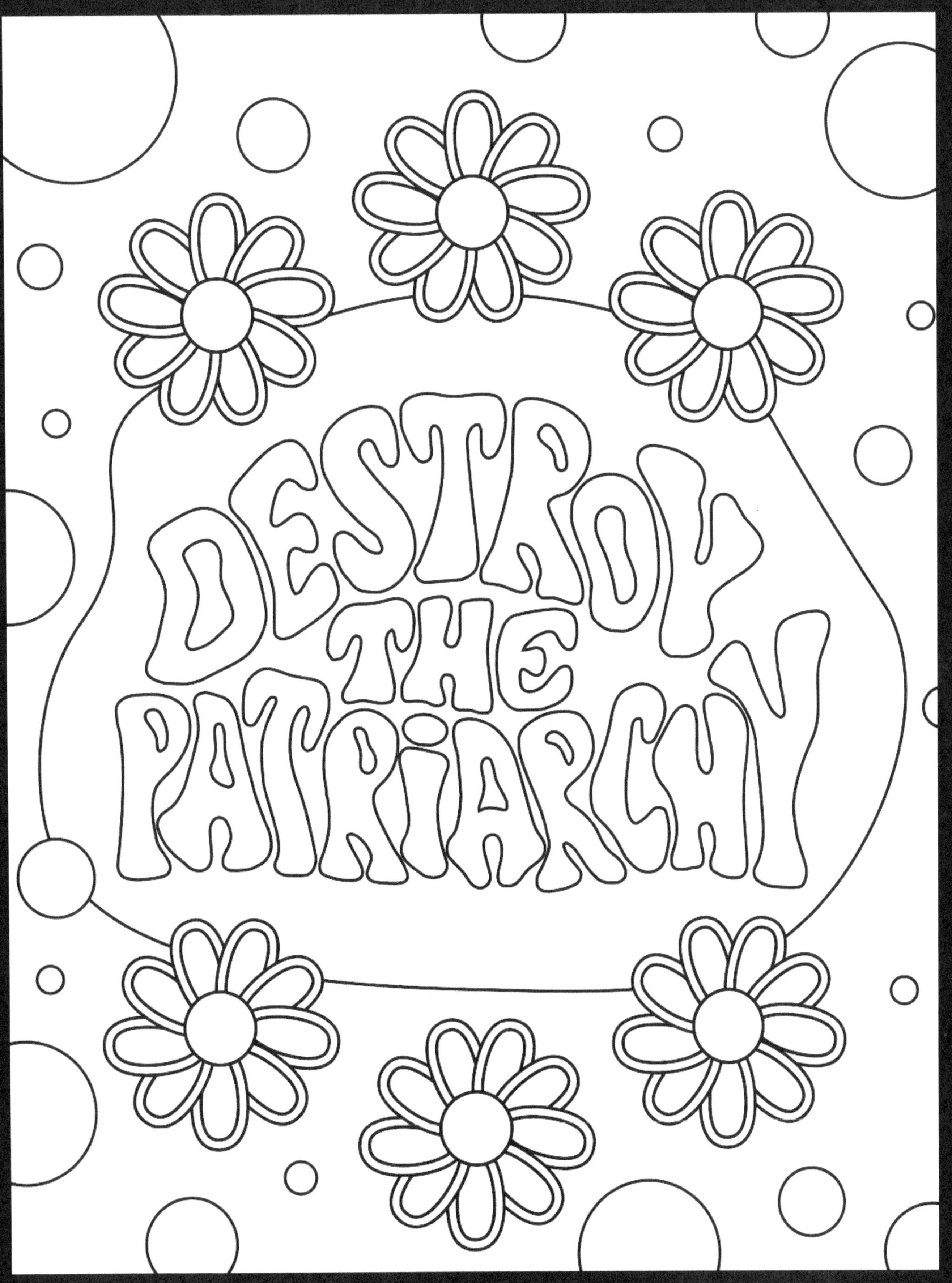

DESTROY THE PATRIARCHY

DESTROY THE PATRIARCHY!

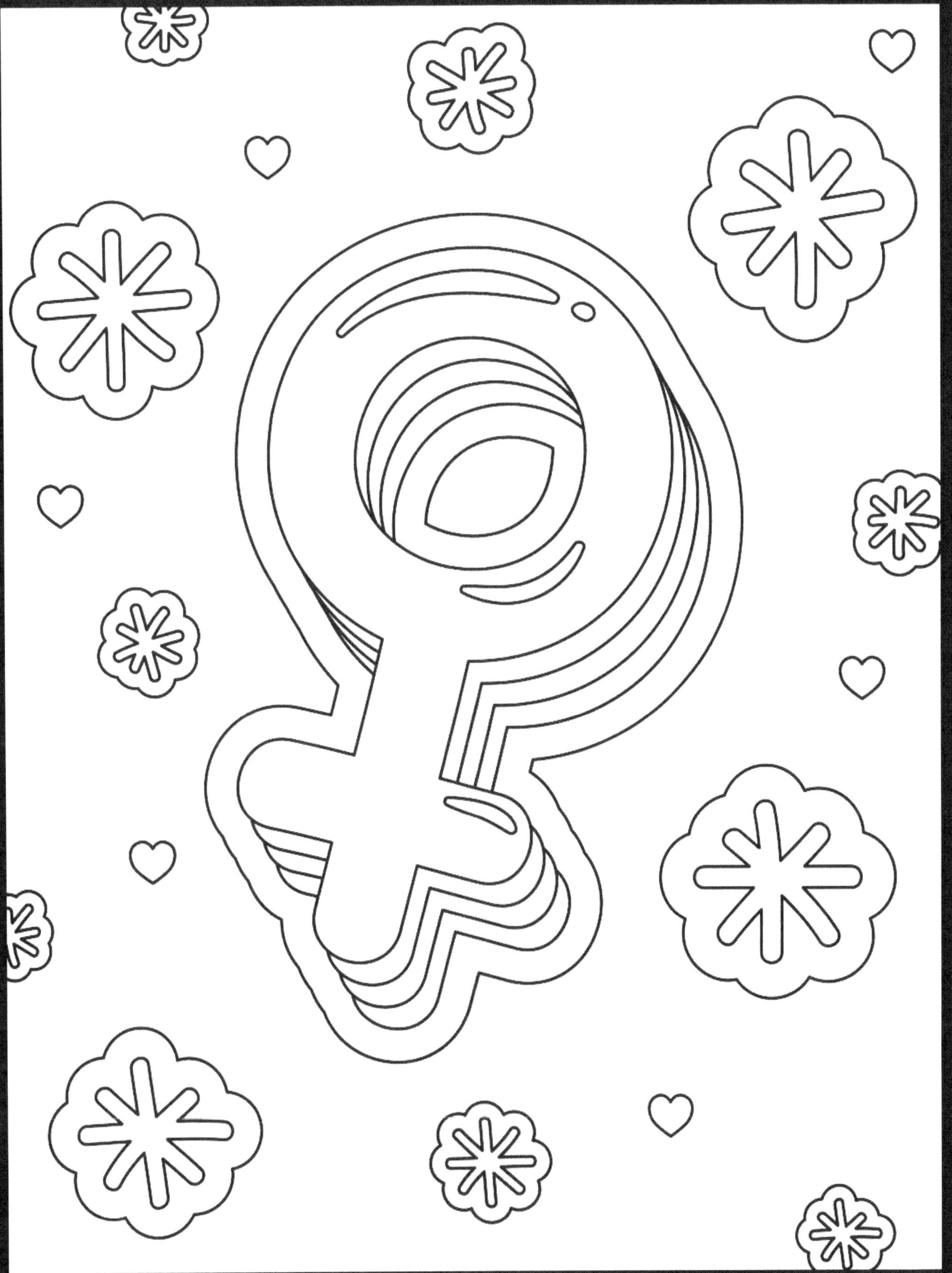

SYMBOLISM

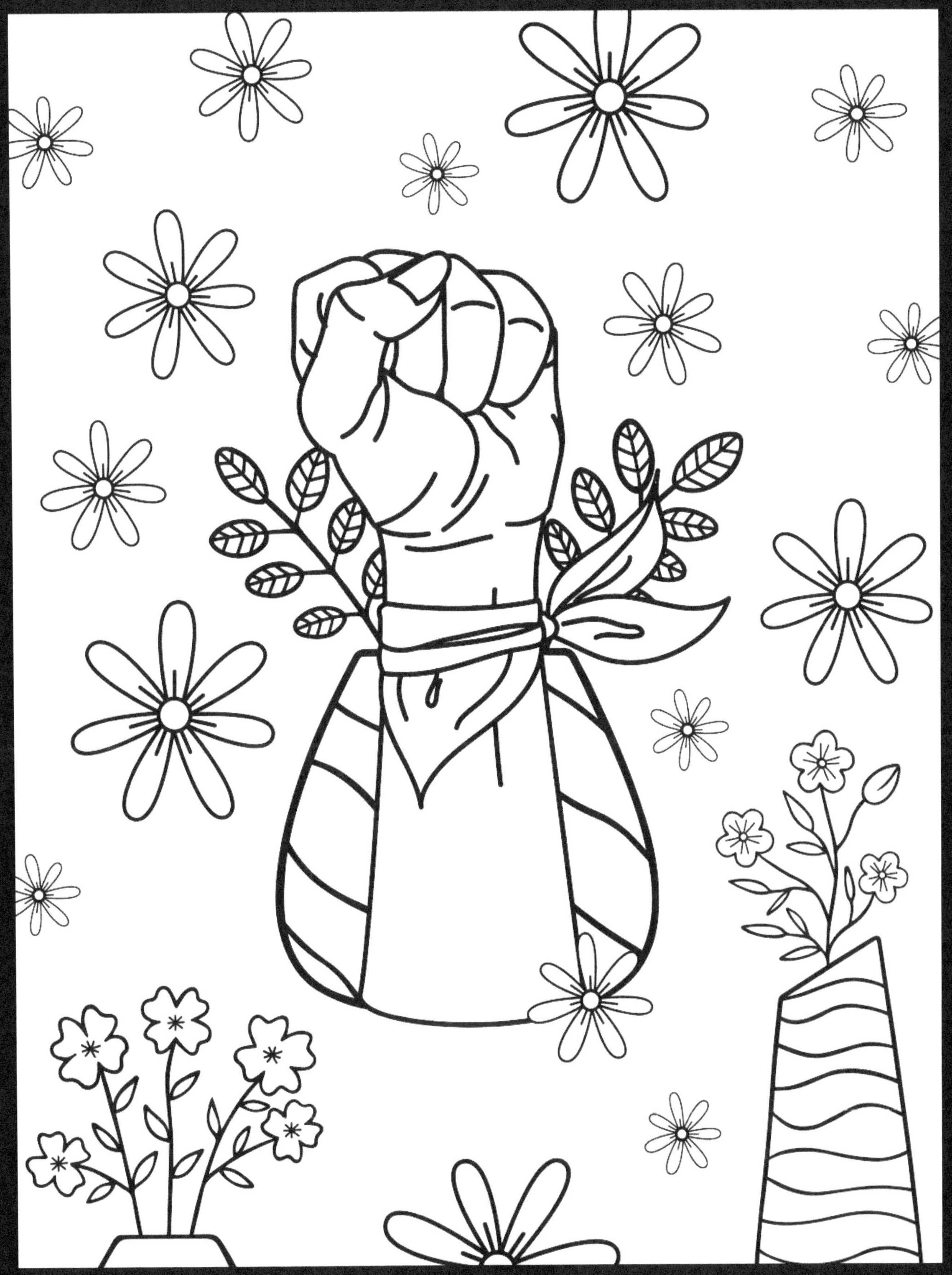

FISTS UP

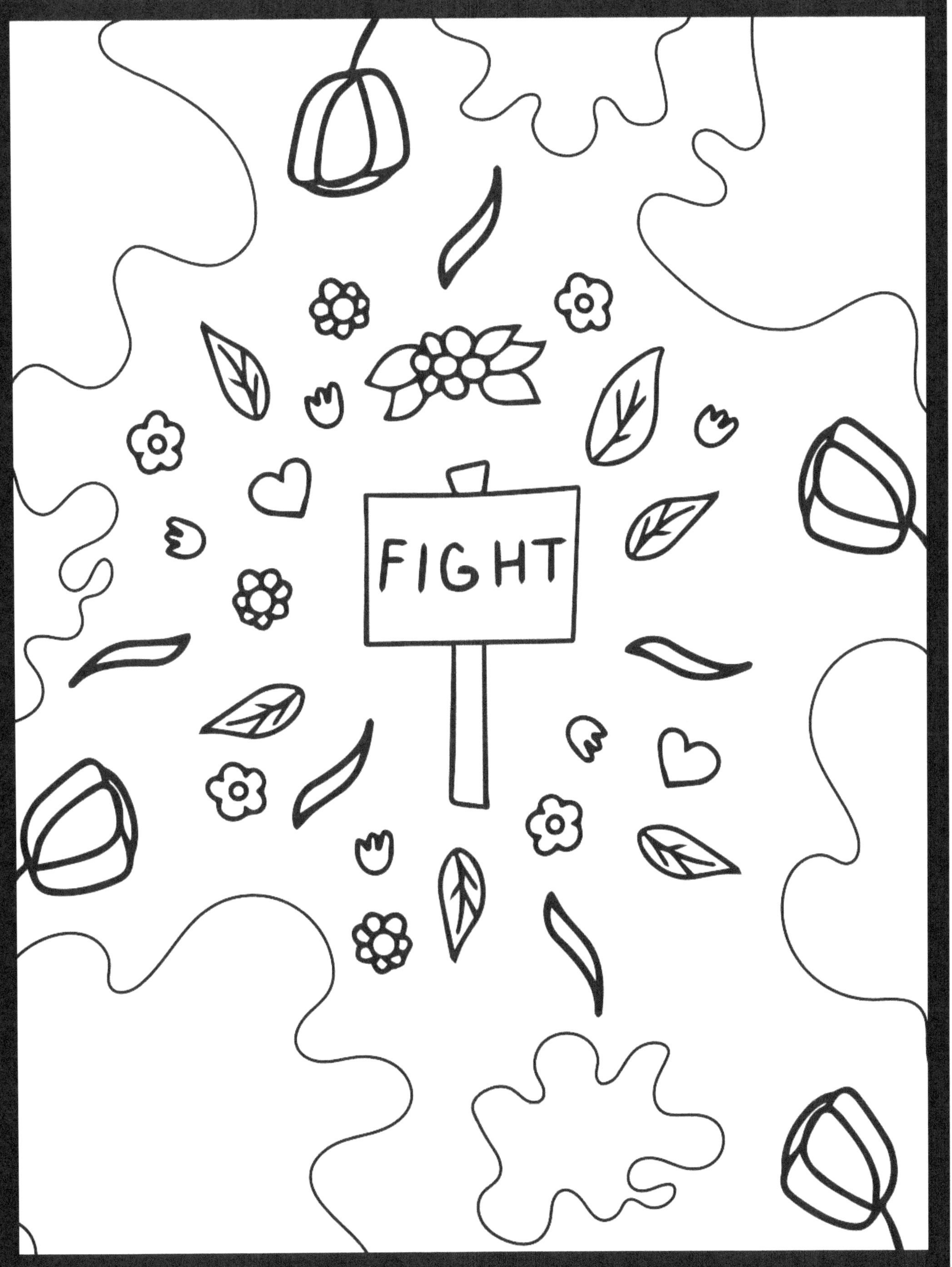
FIGHT

FIGHT

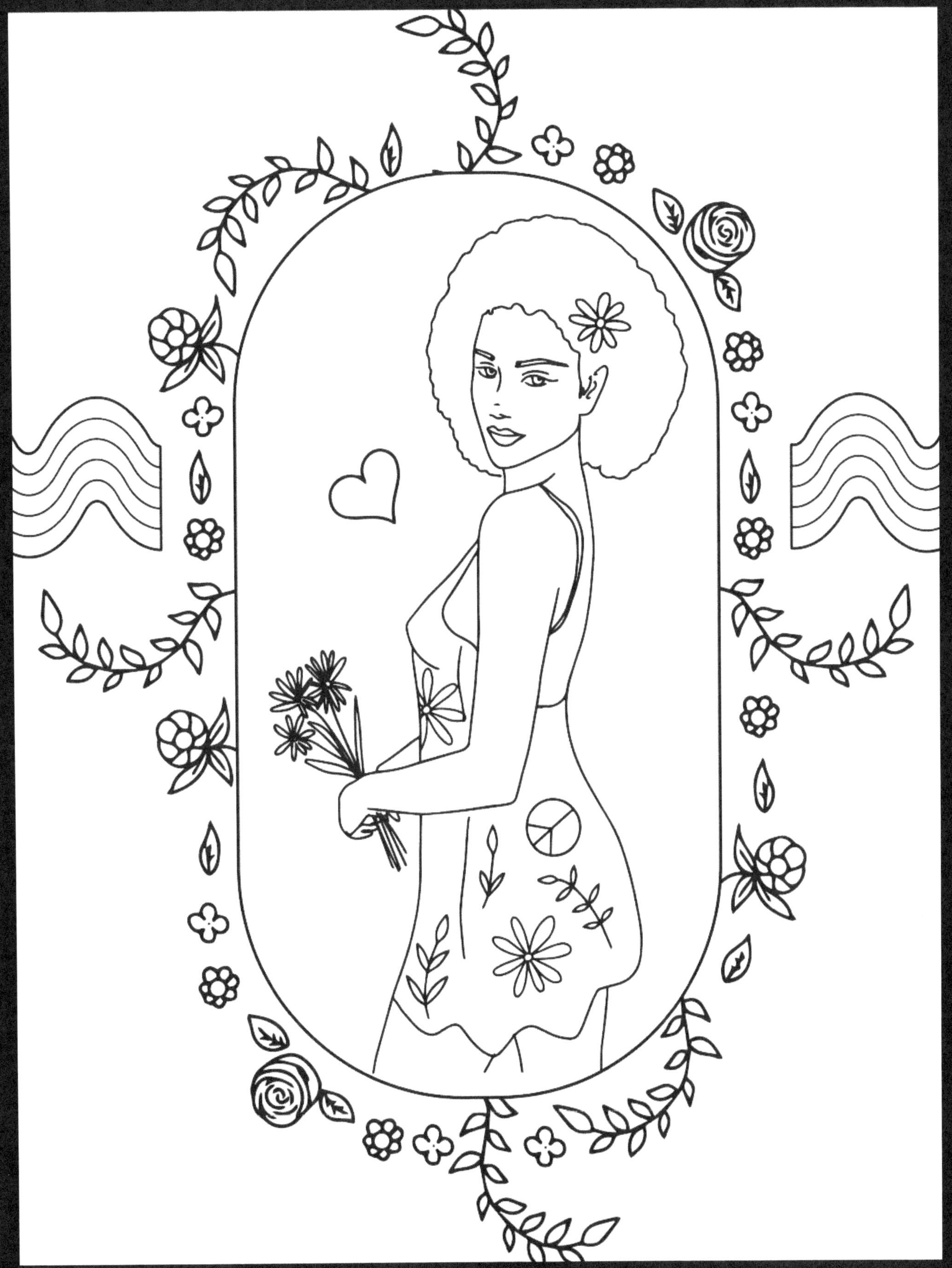

FEMININE BEAUTY

FLOWERING

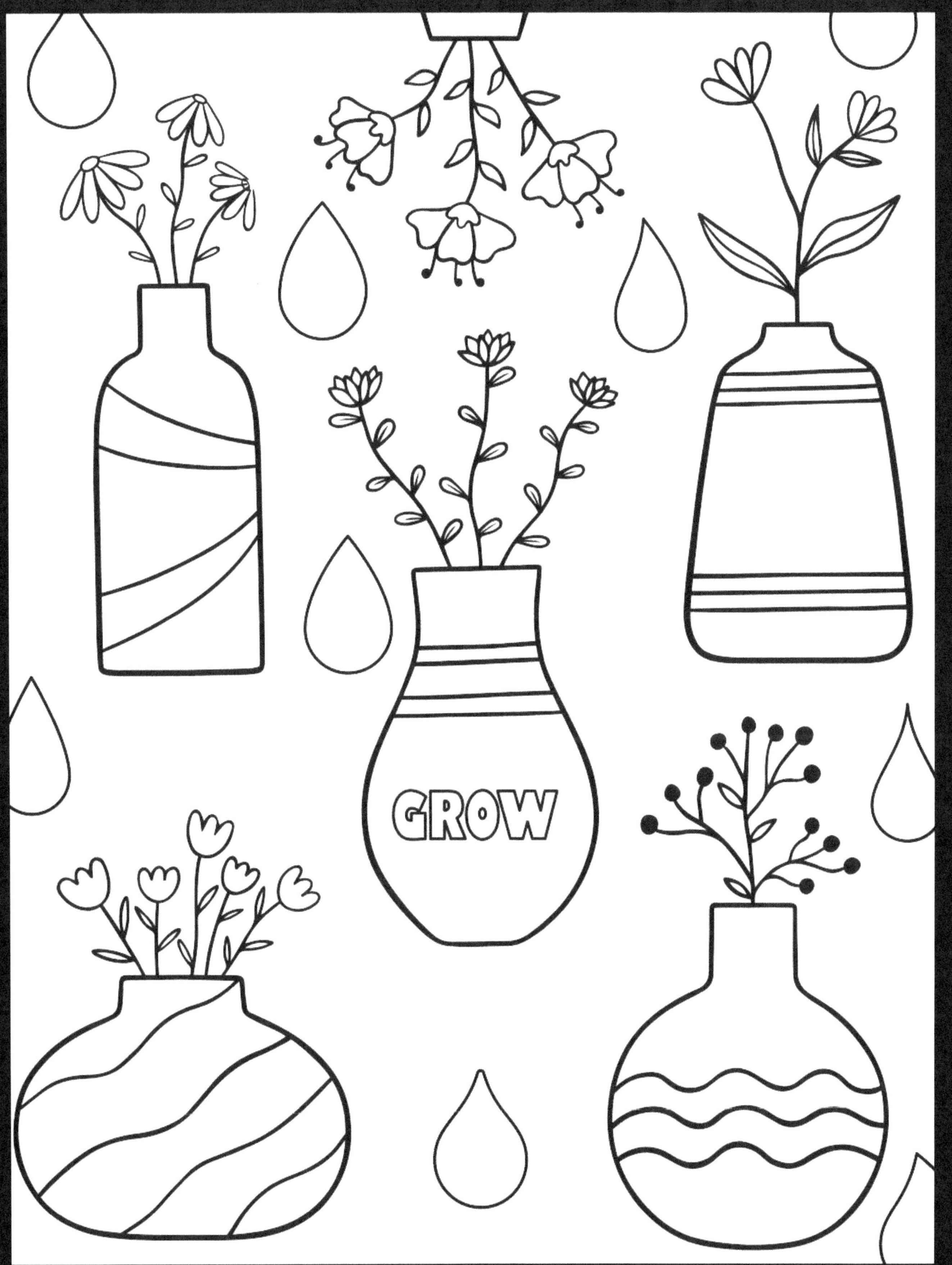
GROW

USE IT TO GROW

USE IT TO GROW

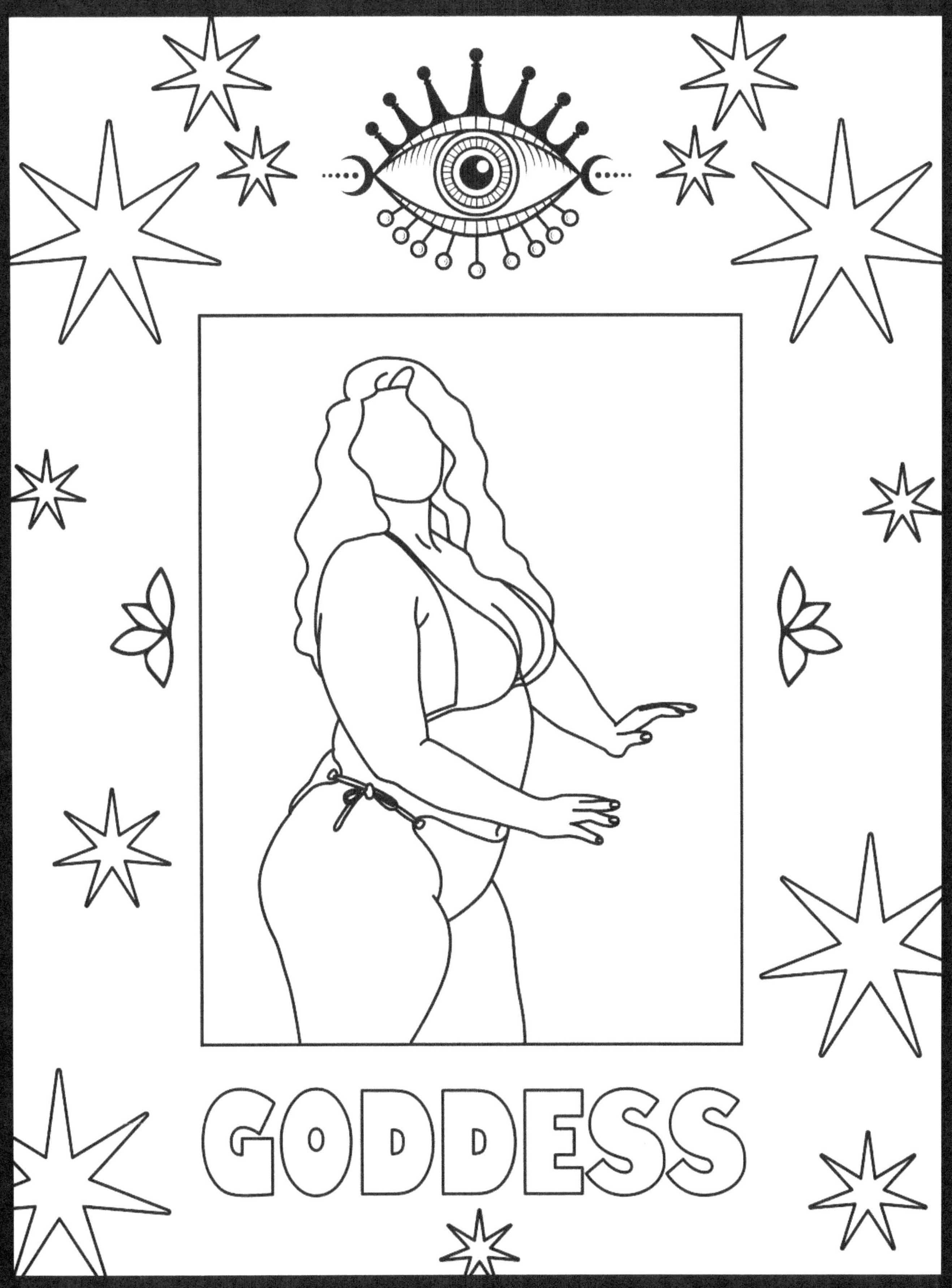

GODDESS

GODDESS

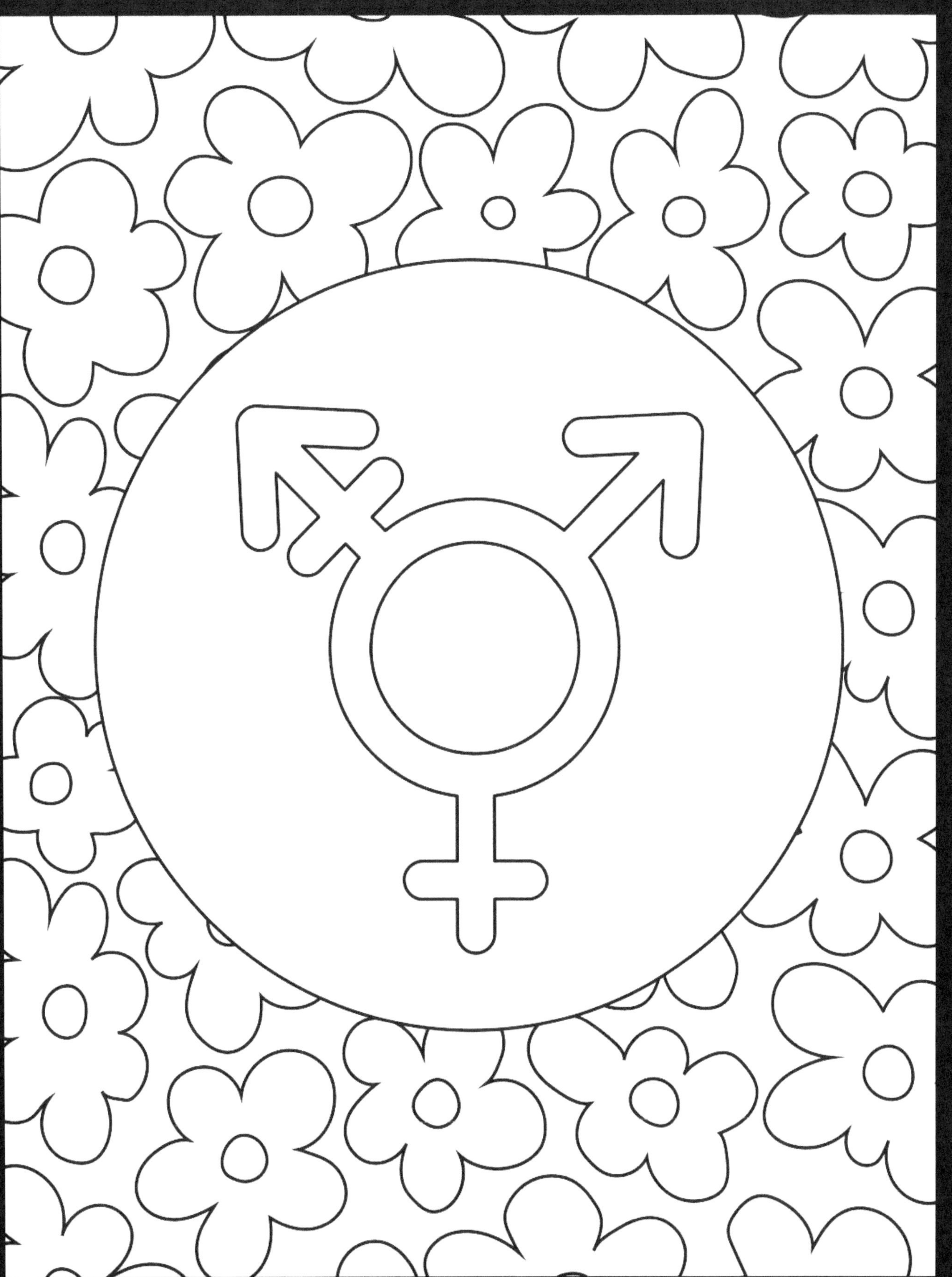

ALL OF US

ALL OF US

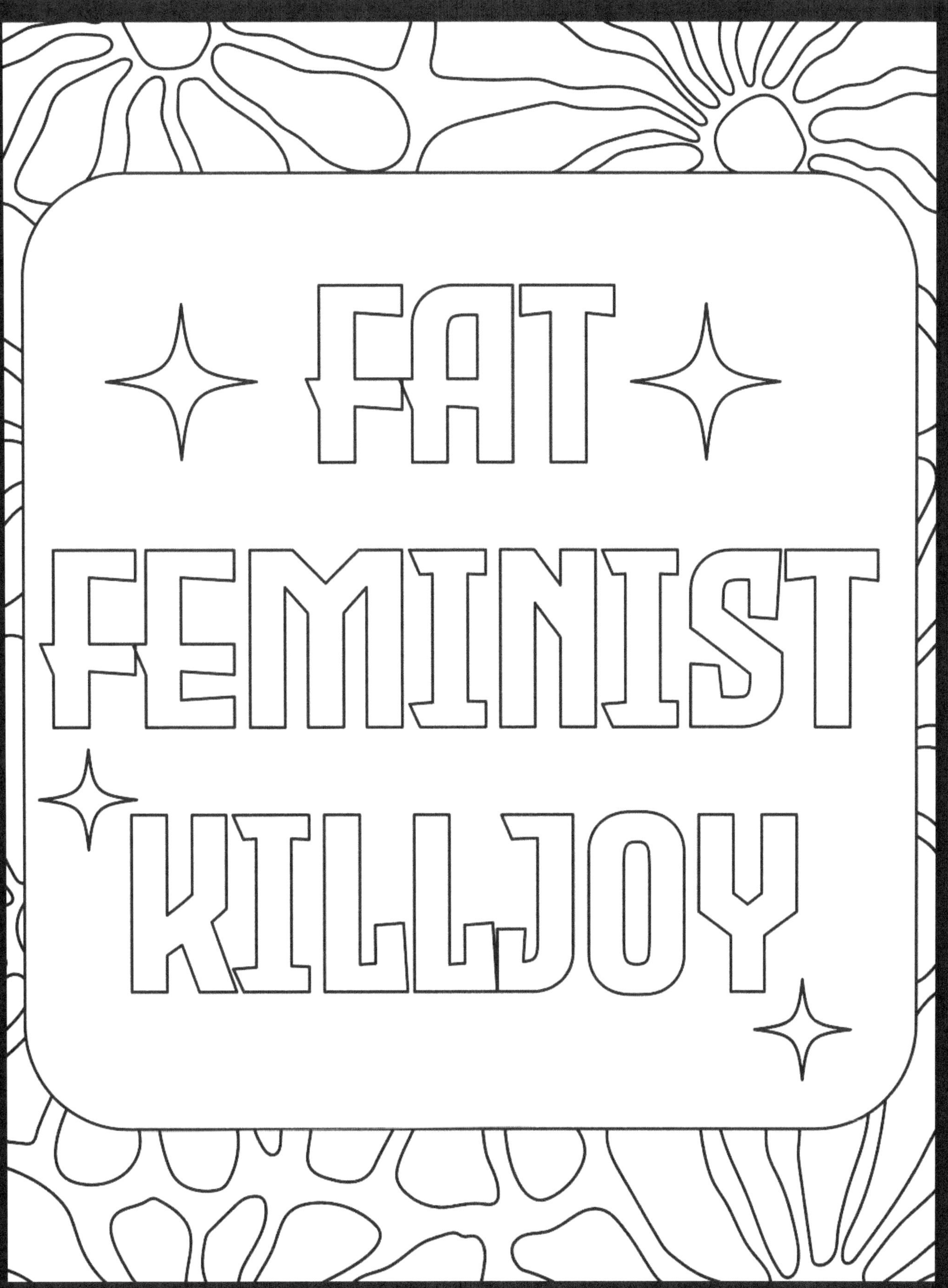

FAT
FEMINIST
KILLJOY

DEIDRE

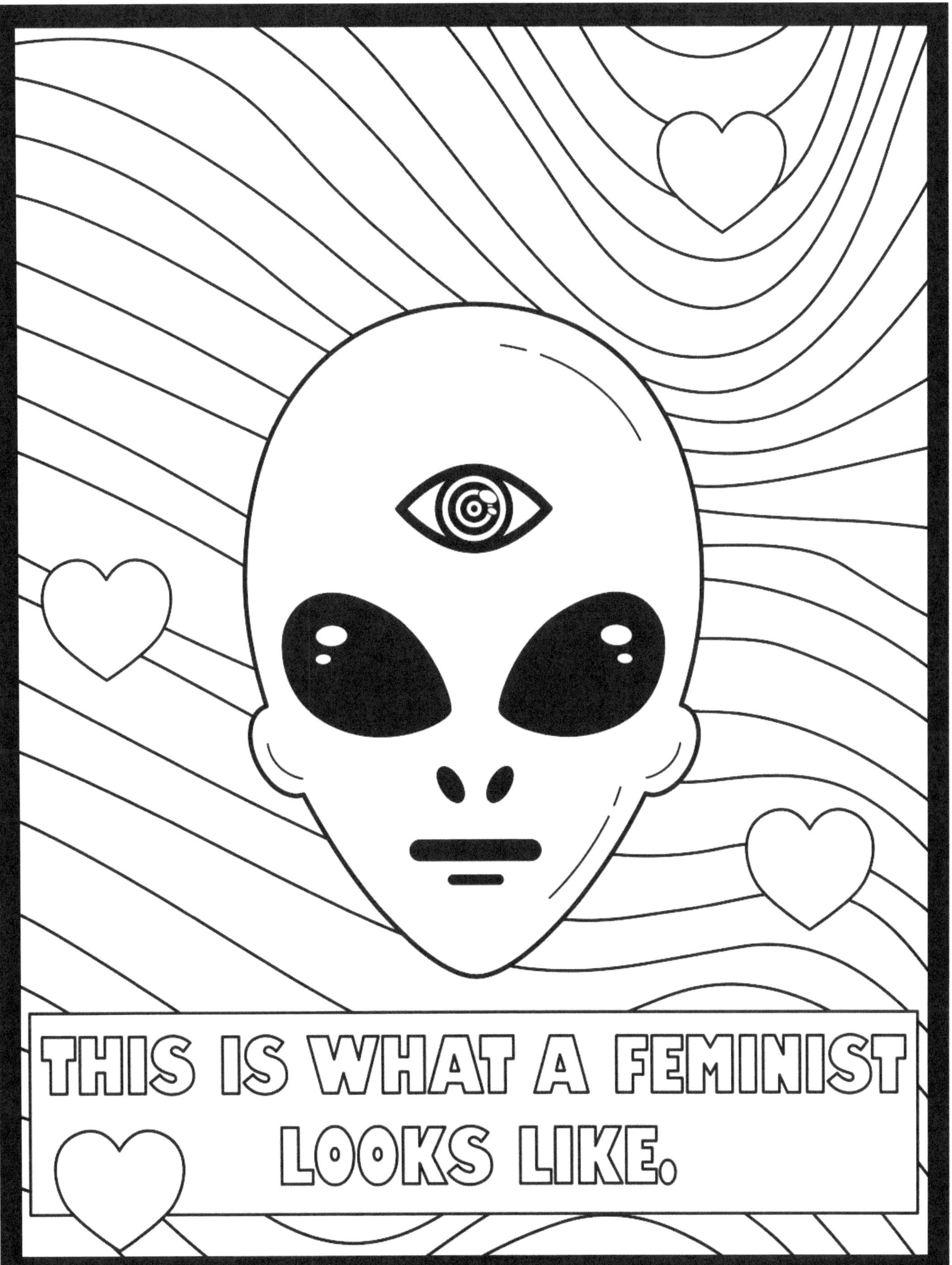

THIS IS WHAT A FEMINIST
LOOKS LIKE.

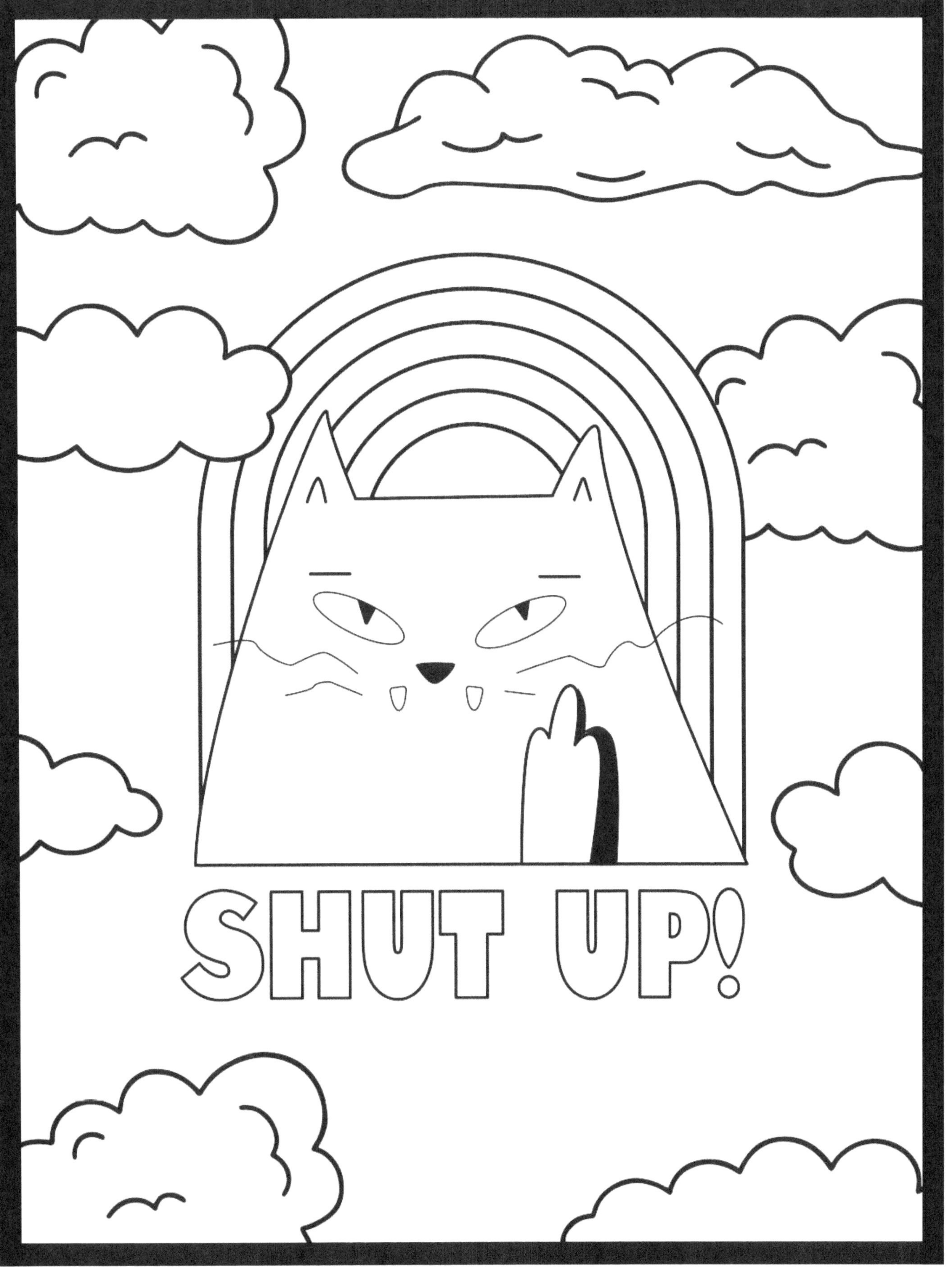
SHUT UP!

THANK YOU VERY MUCH

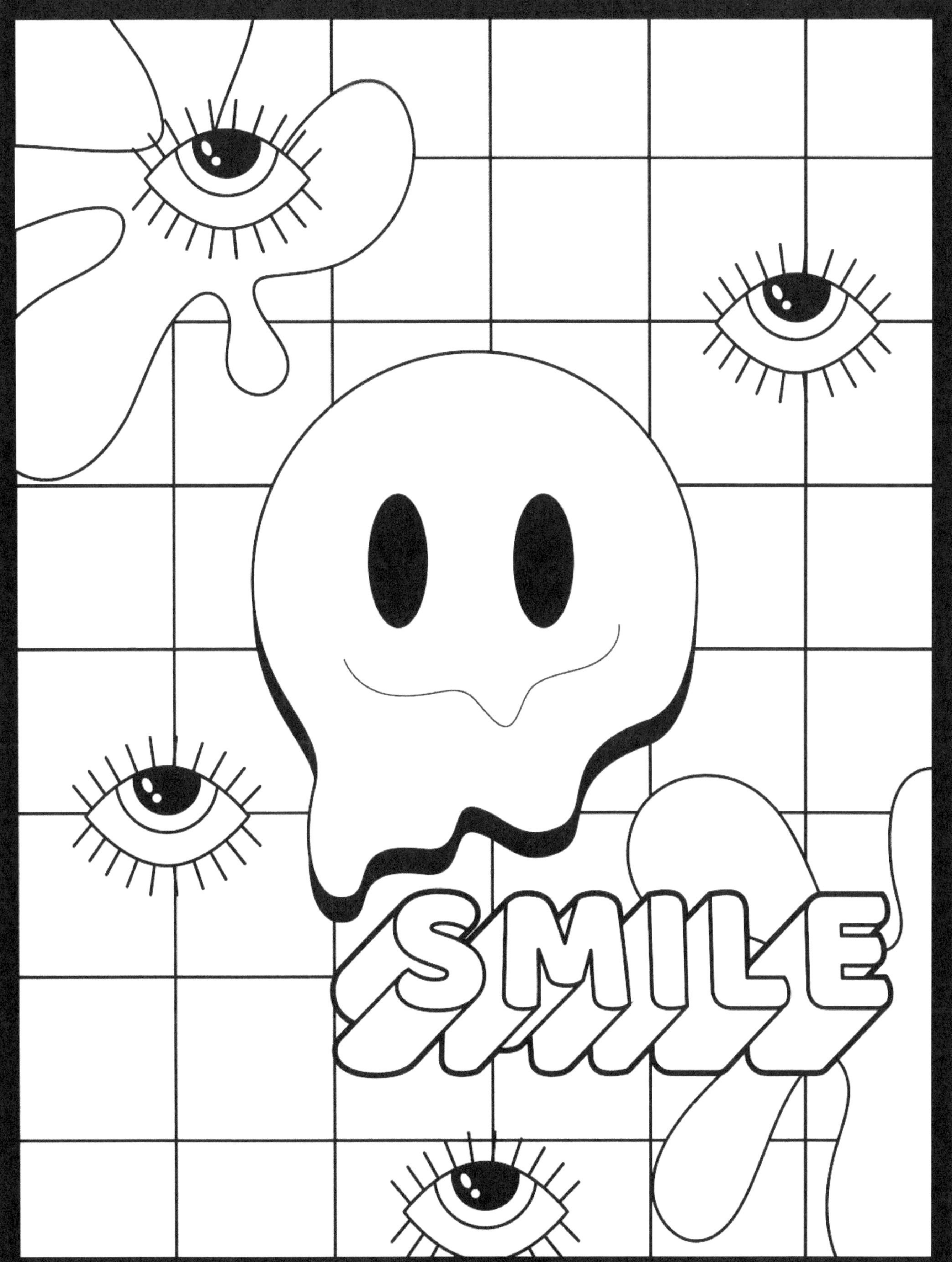

SMILE

IF YOU WANT TO

IF YOU WANT TO

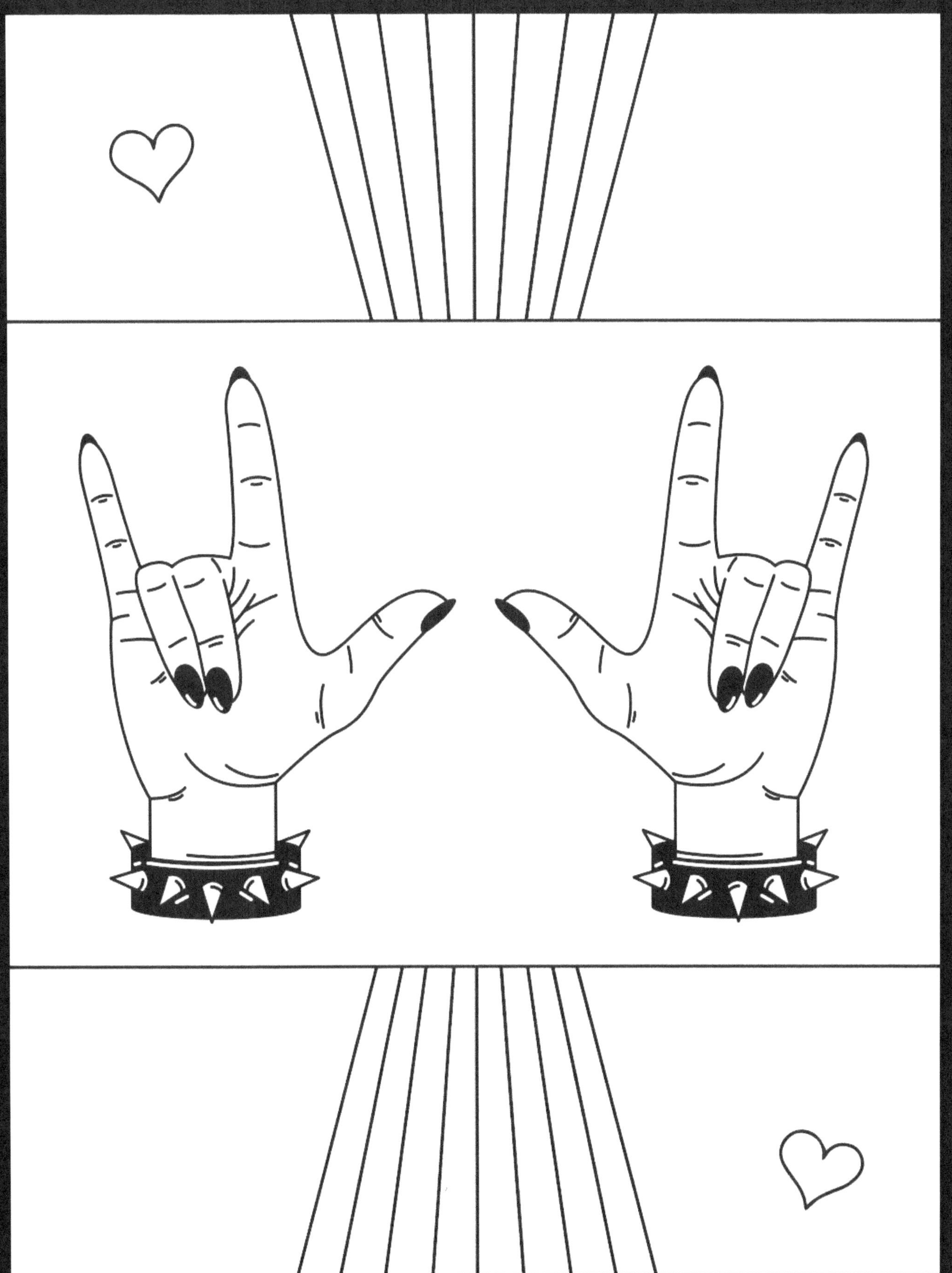

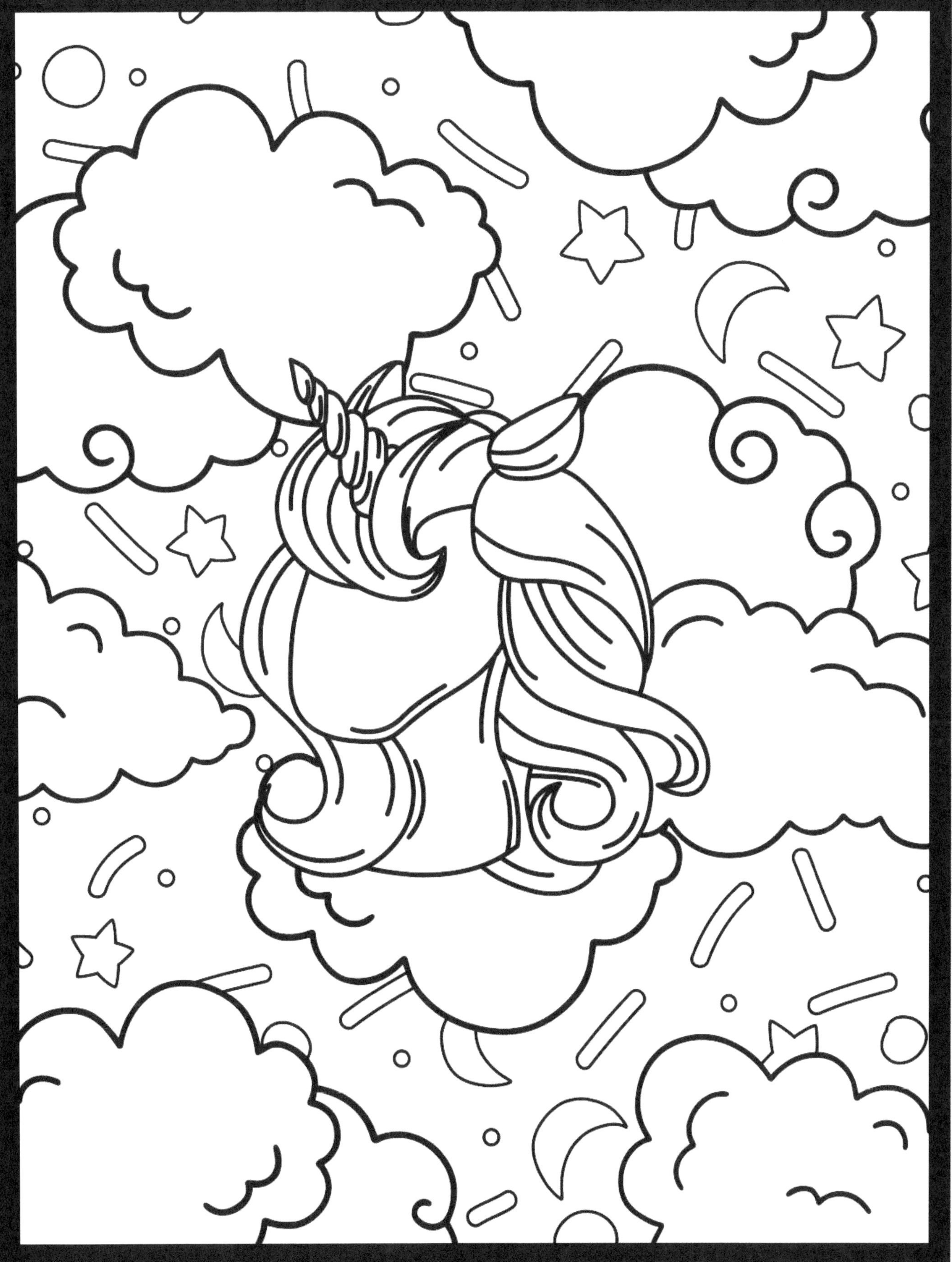

MAGICAL CREATURES

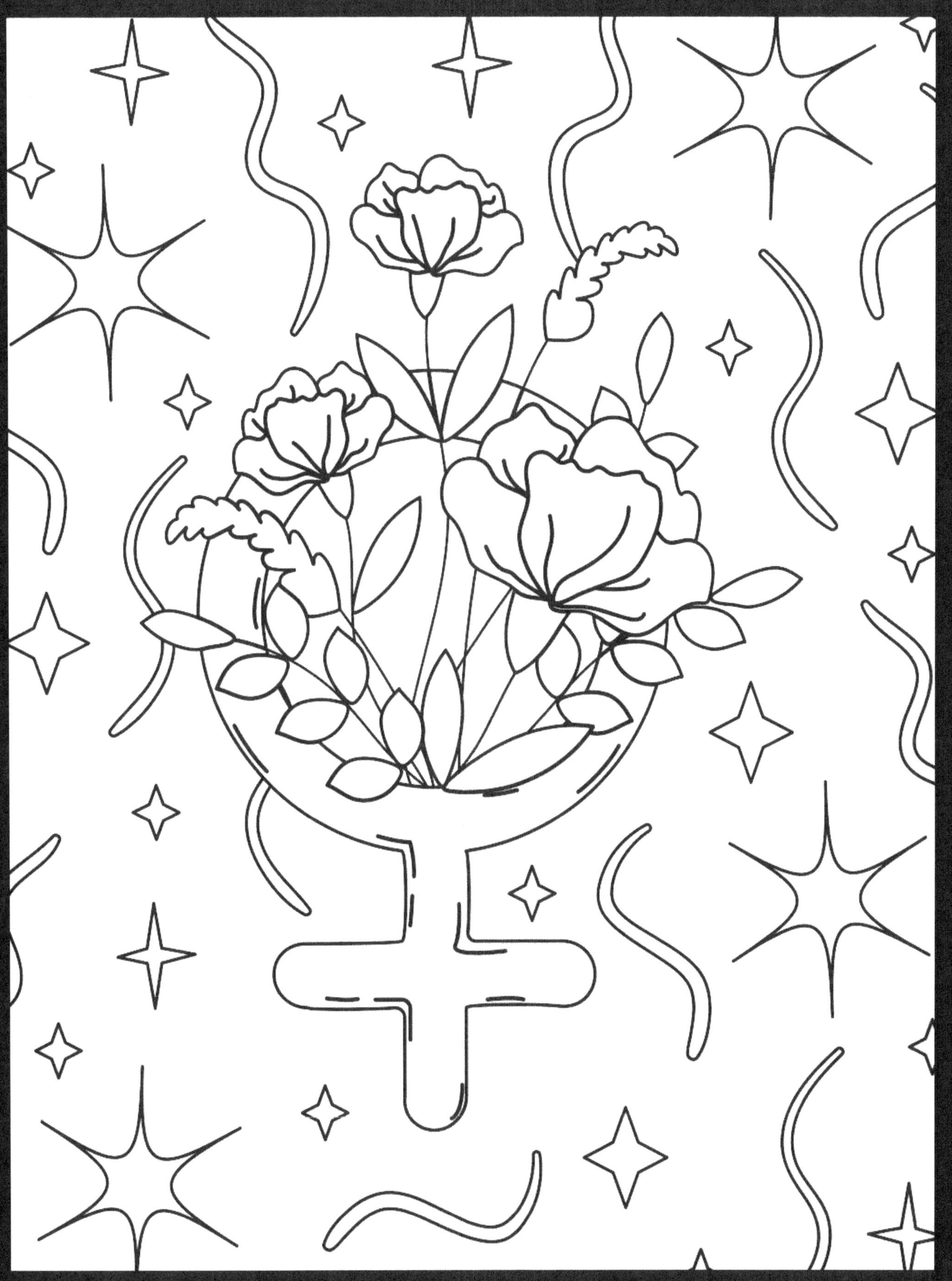

NOT FRAGILE LIKE FLOWERS

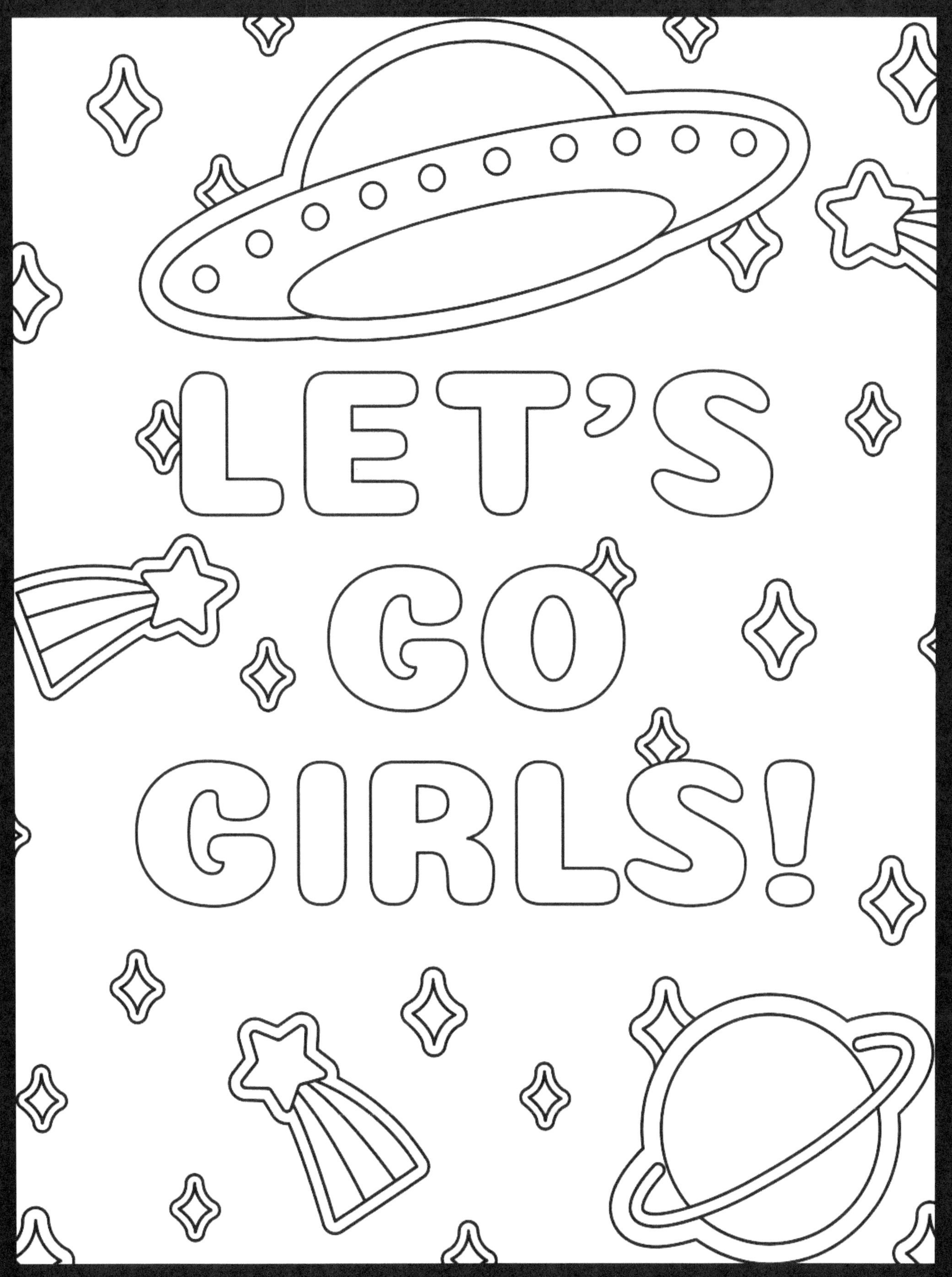
LET'S
GO
GIRLS!

WE'RE OUT OF HERE

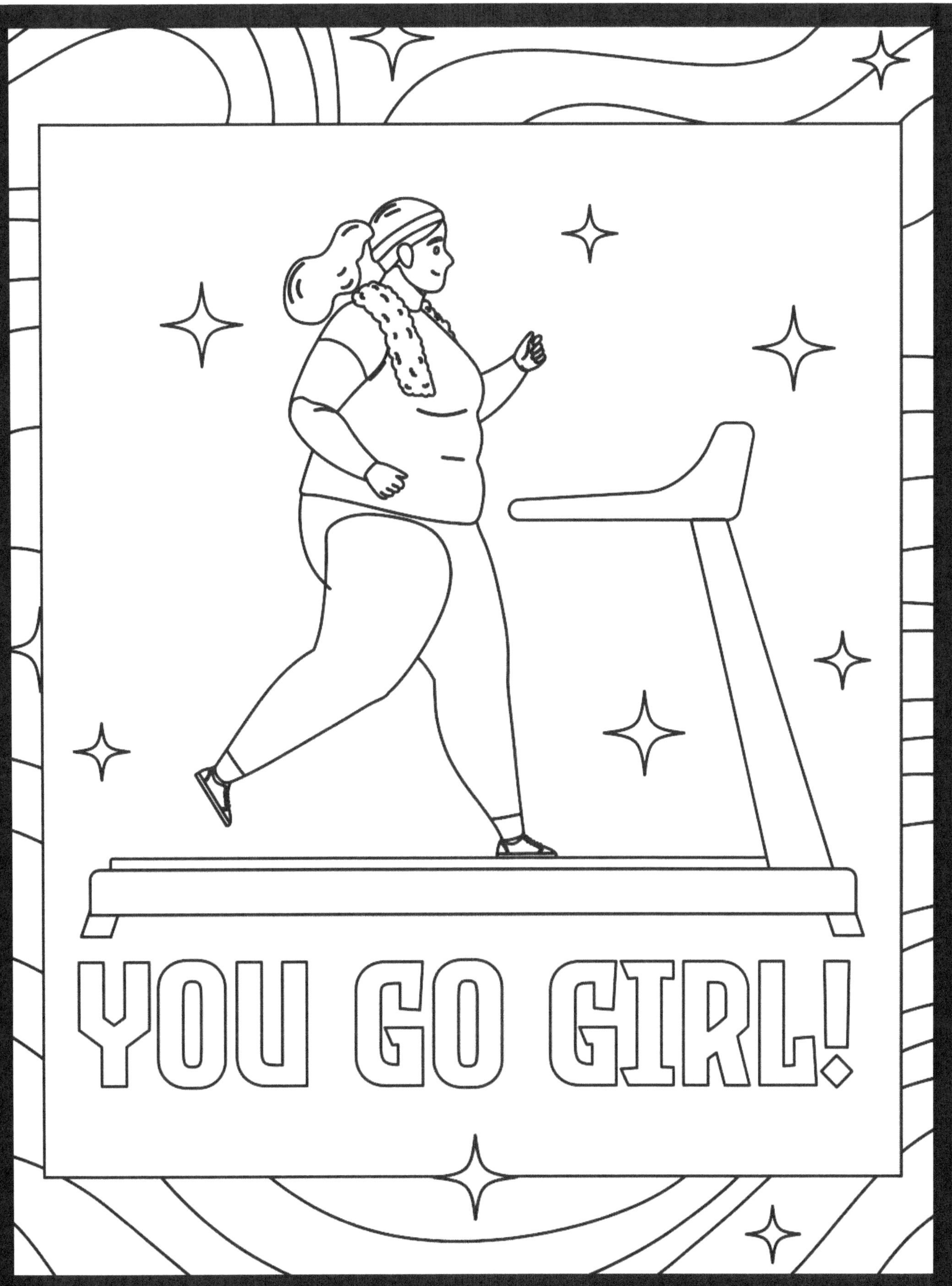
YOU GO GIRL!

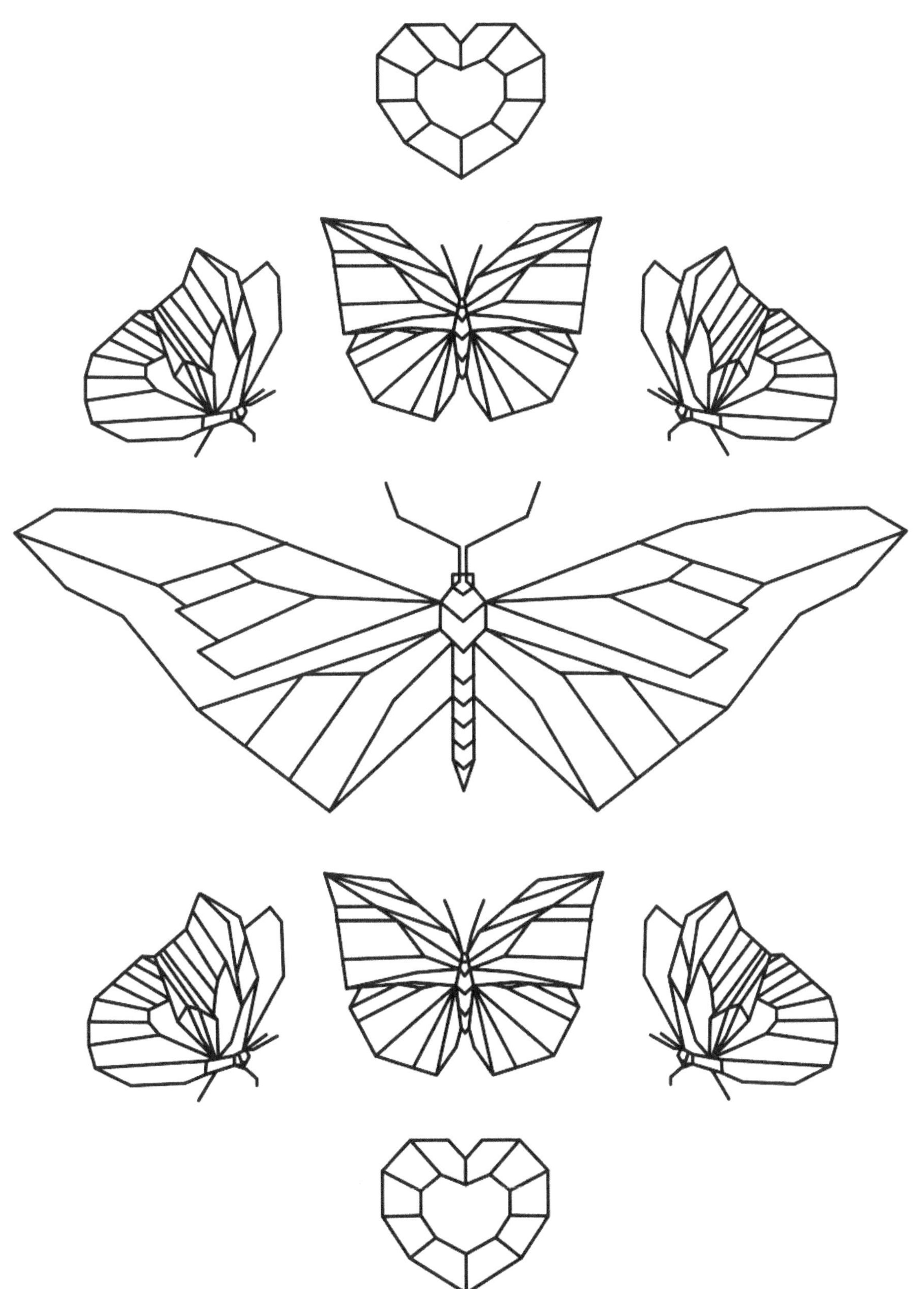

METAMORPHOSIS

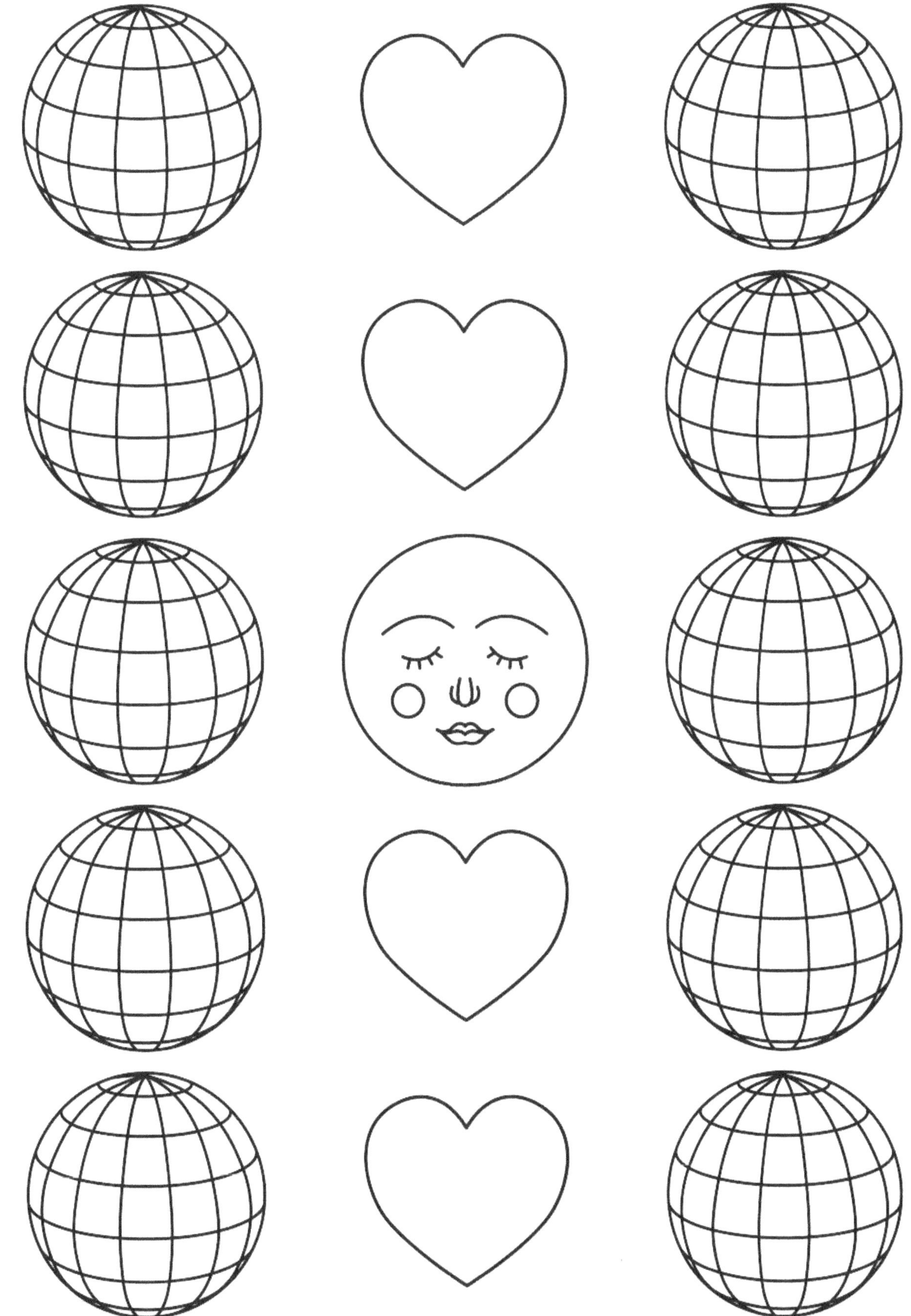

MOTHER EARTH

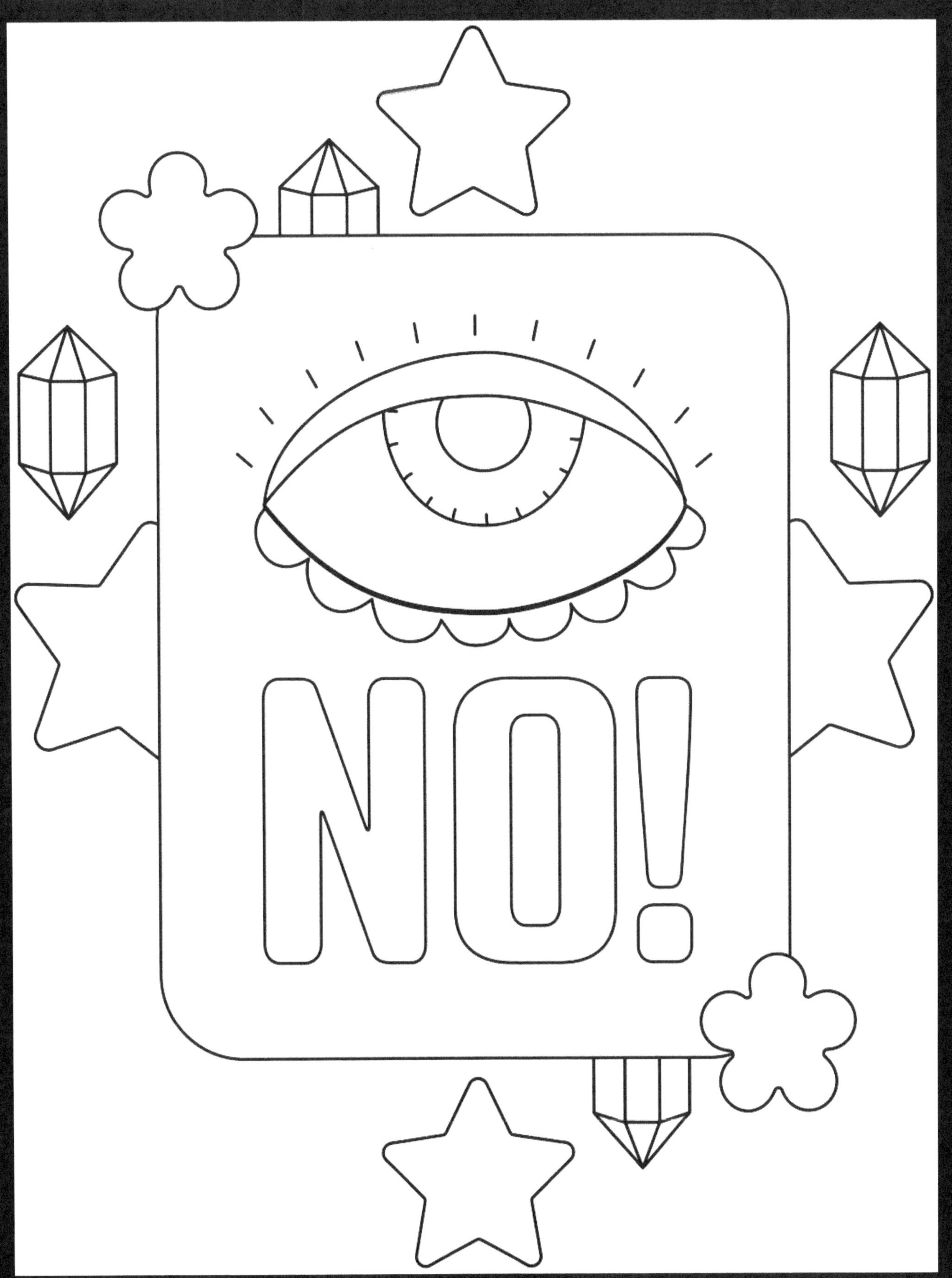
NO!

NO IS A FULL SENTENCE

NO IS A FULL SENTENCE

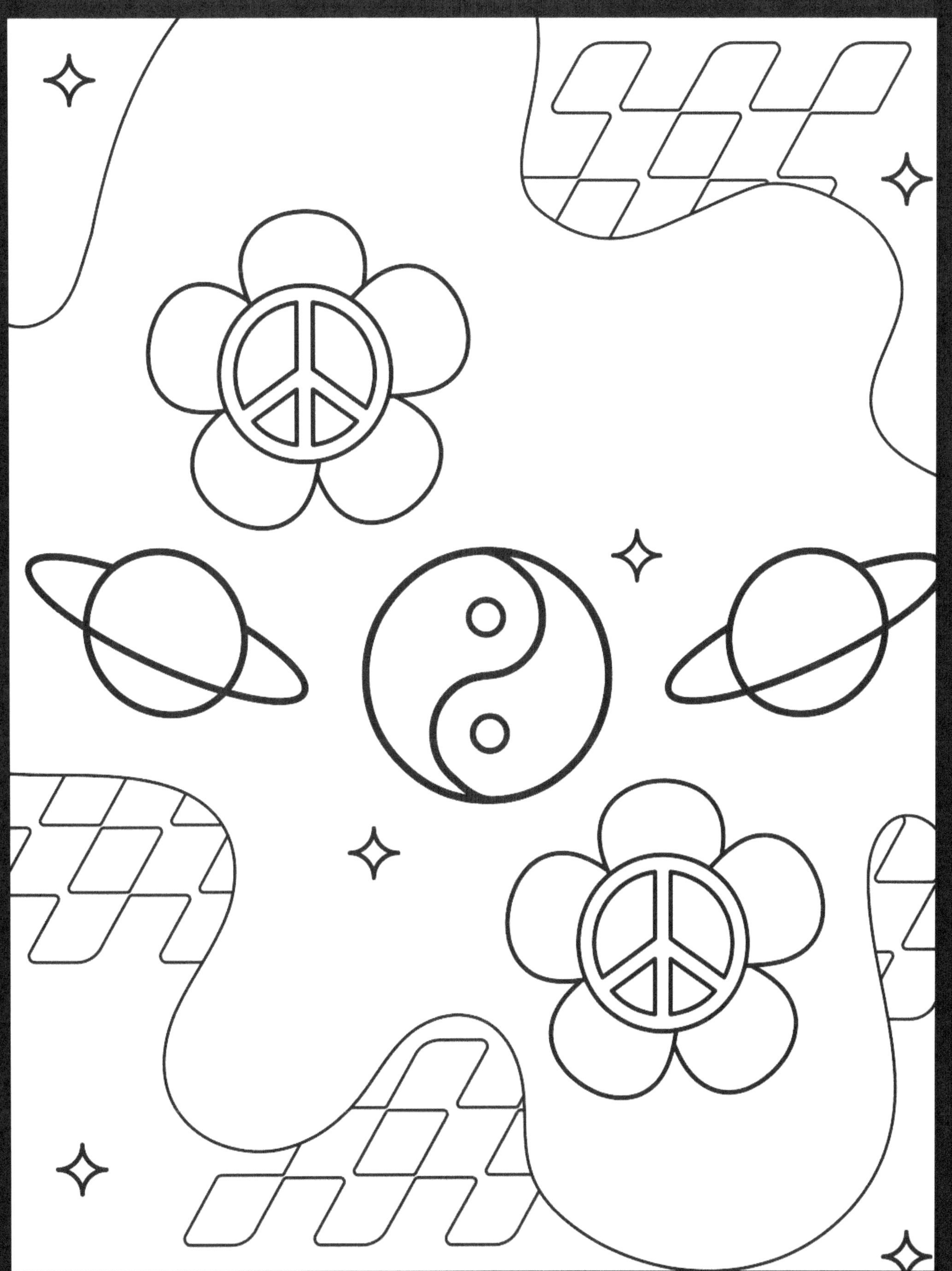

GIVE ME SPACE.

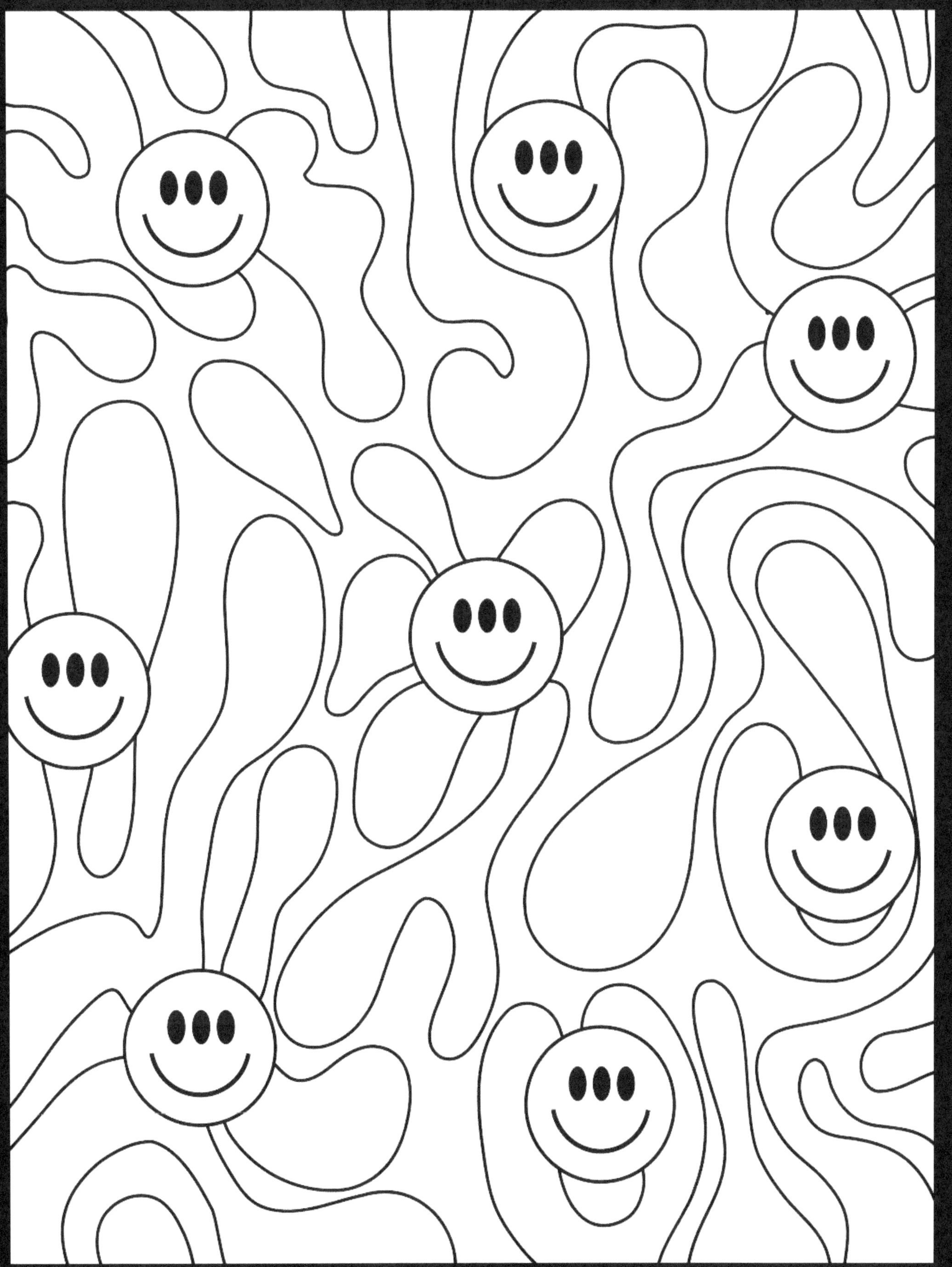

THIRD EYE

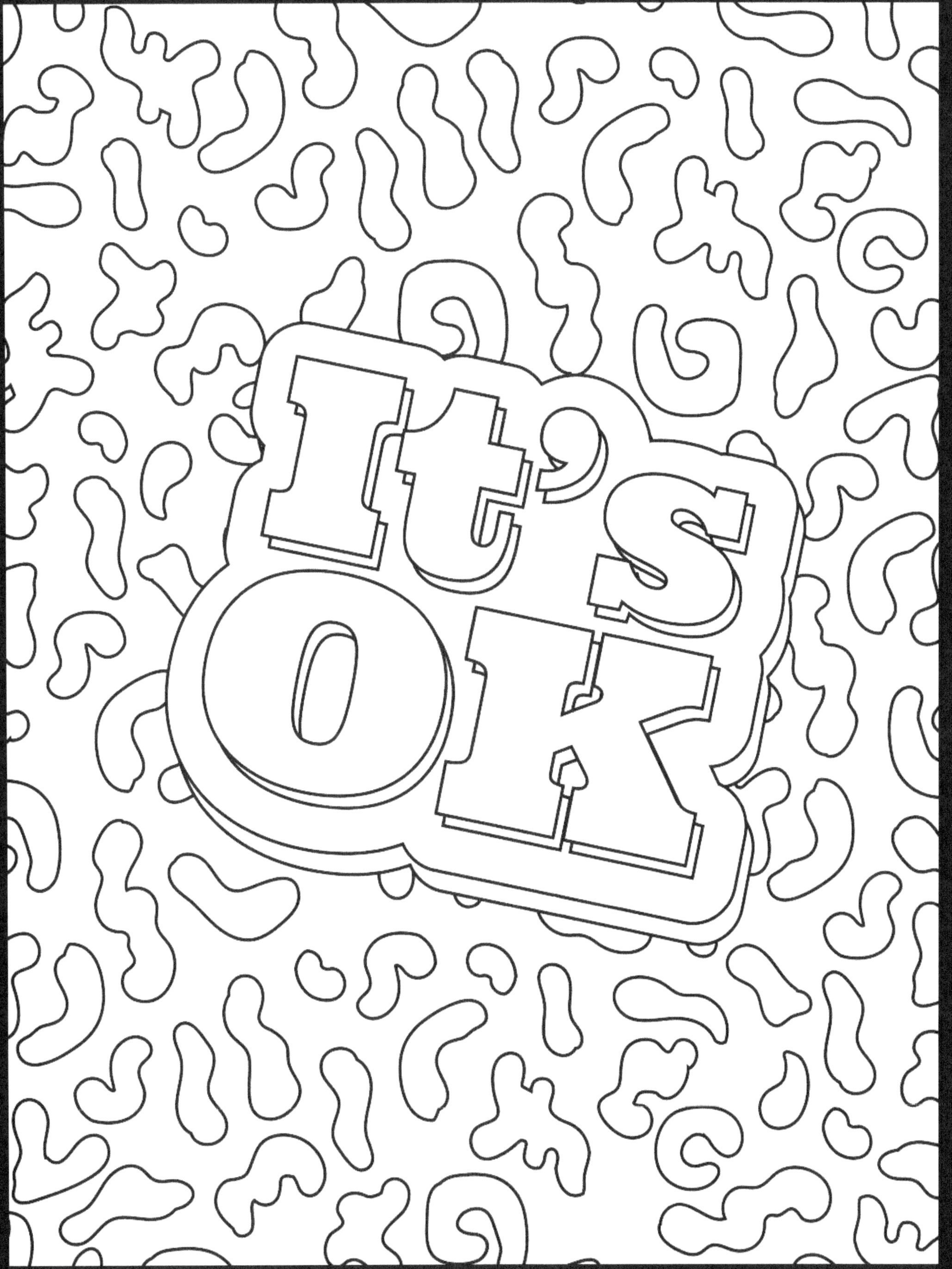
It's
OK

IT IS I PROMISE.

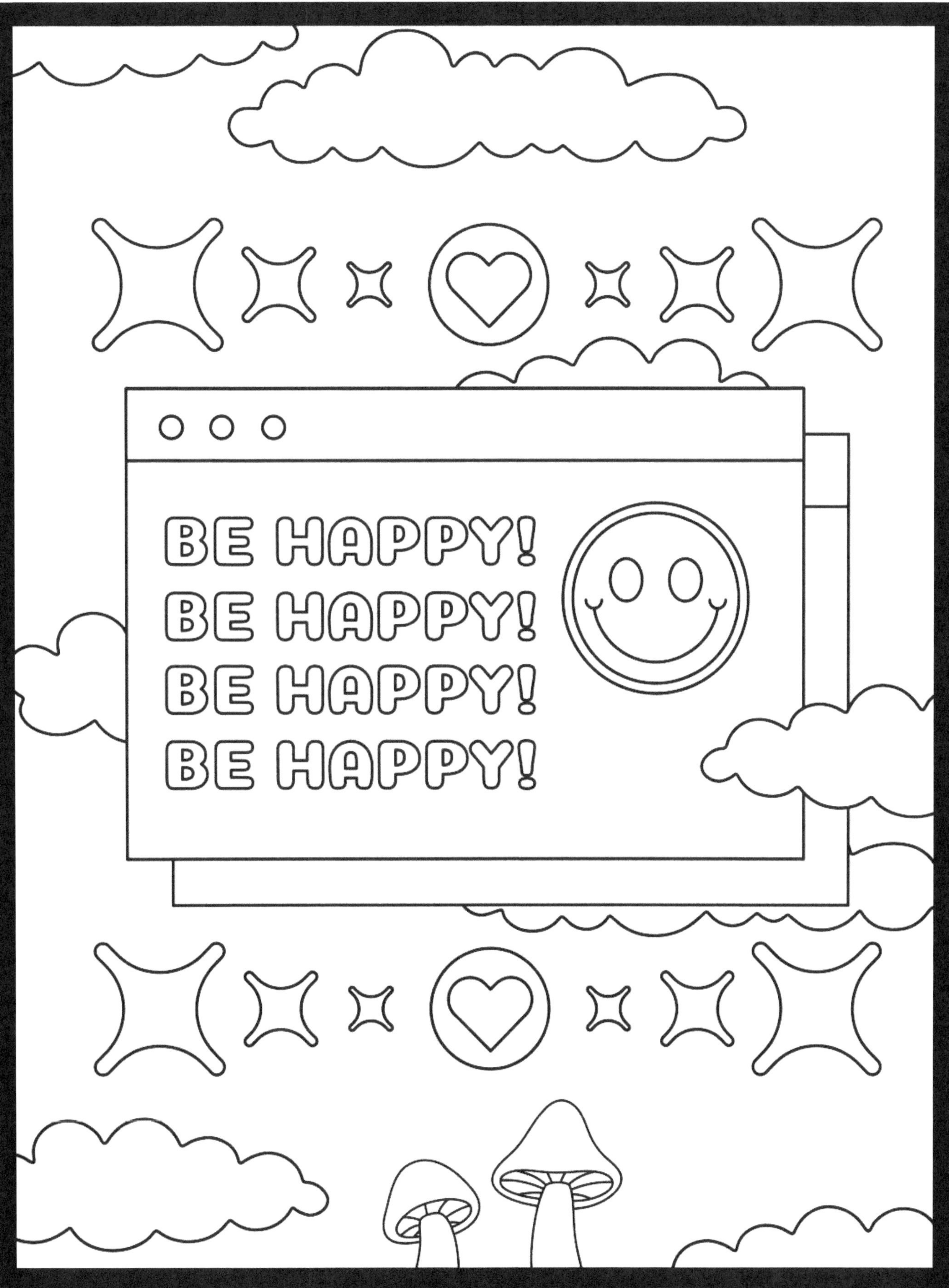

BE HAPPY!
BE HAPPY!
BE HAPPY!
BE HAPPY!

TRYING OUR BEST

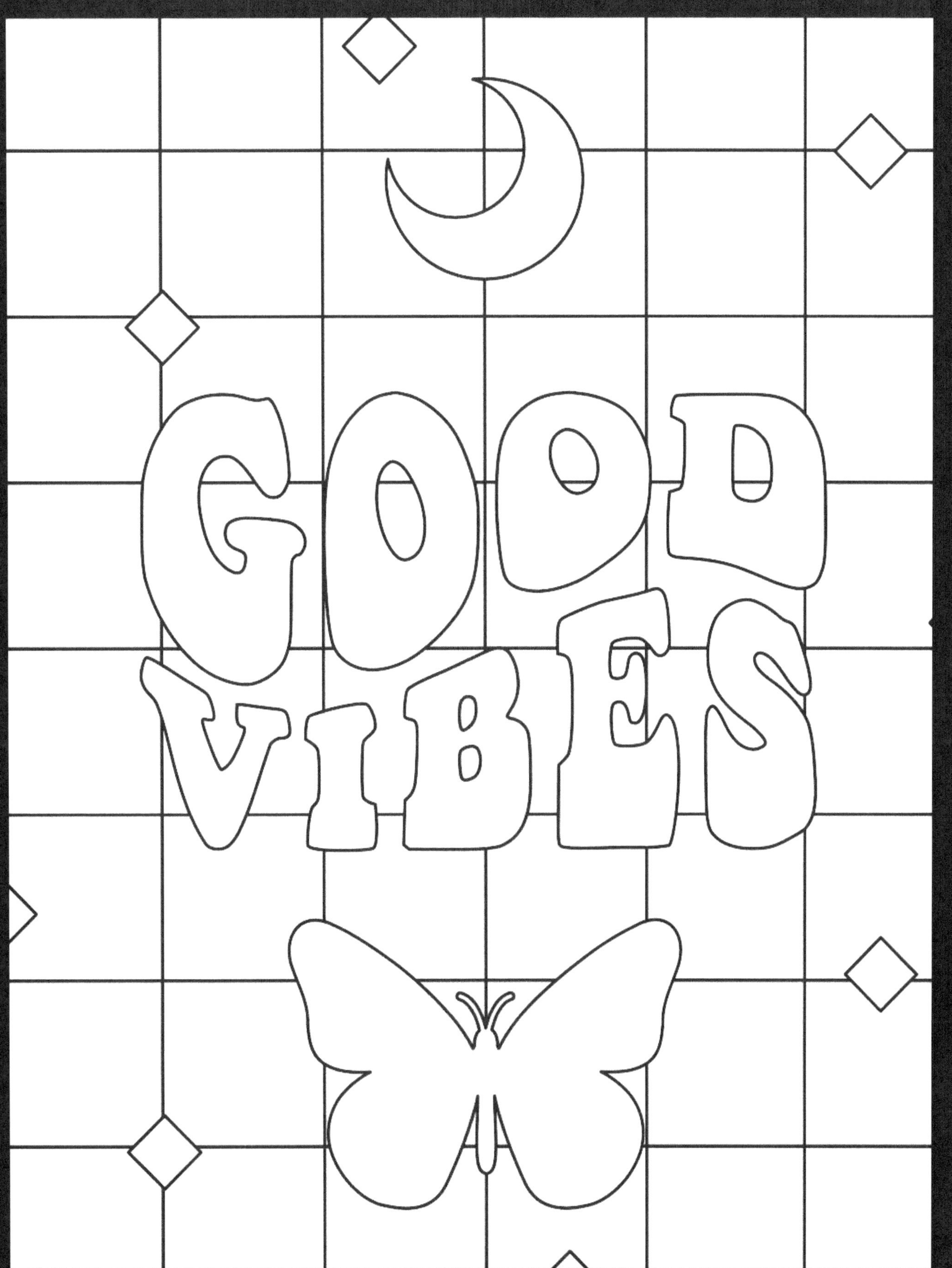

GOOD VIBES

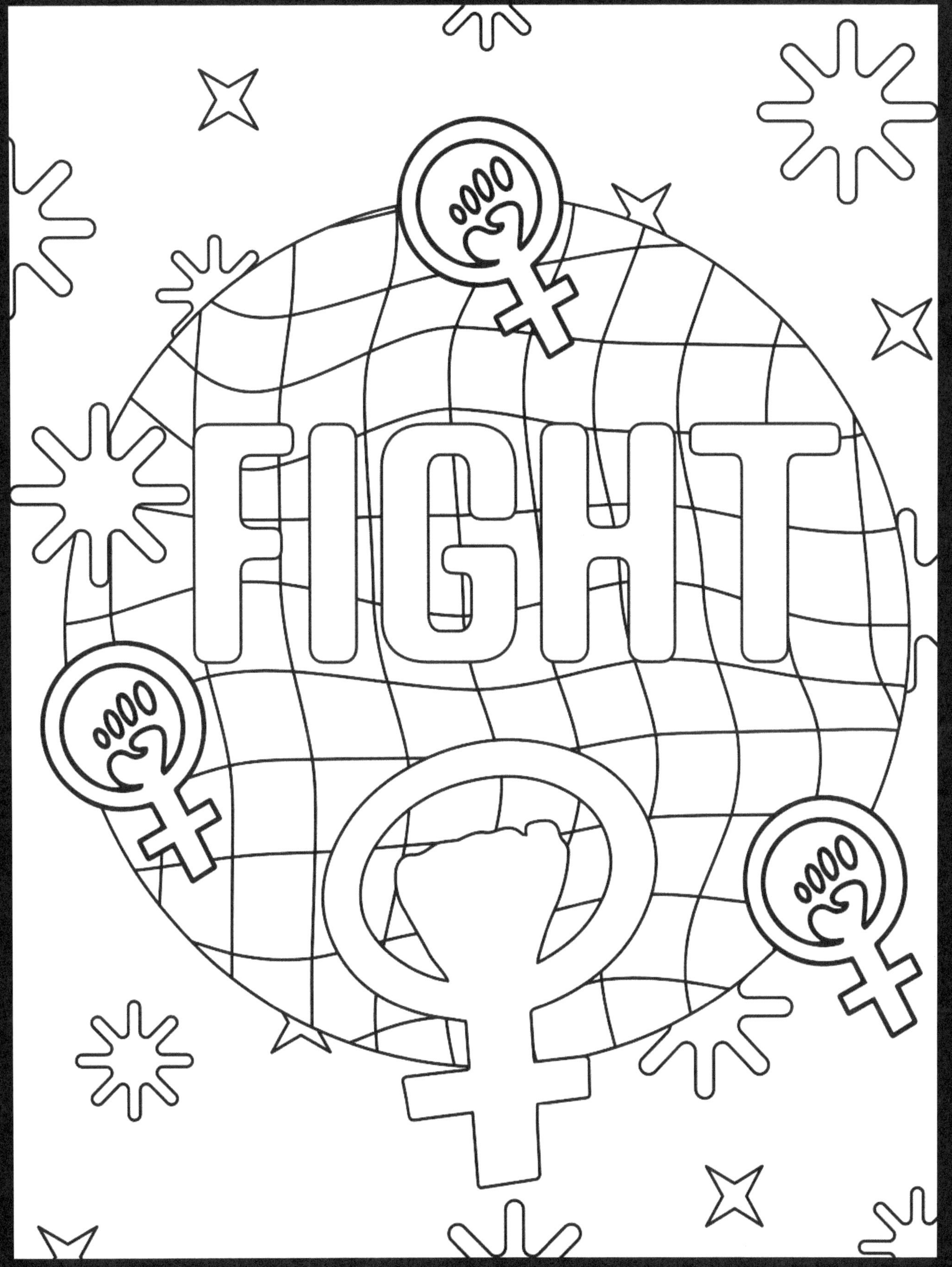
FIGHT

FIGHT LIKE THE SUFFRAGETTES

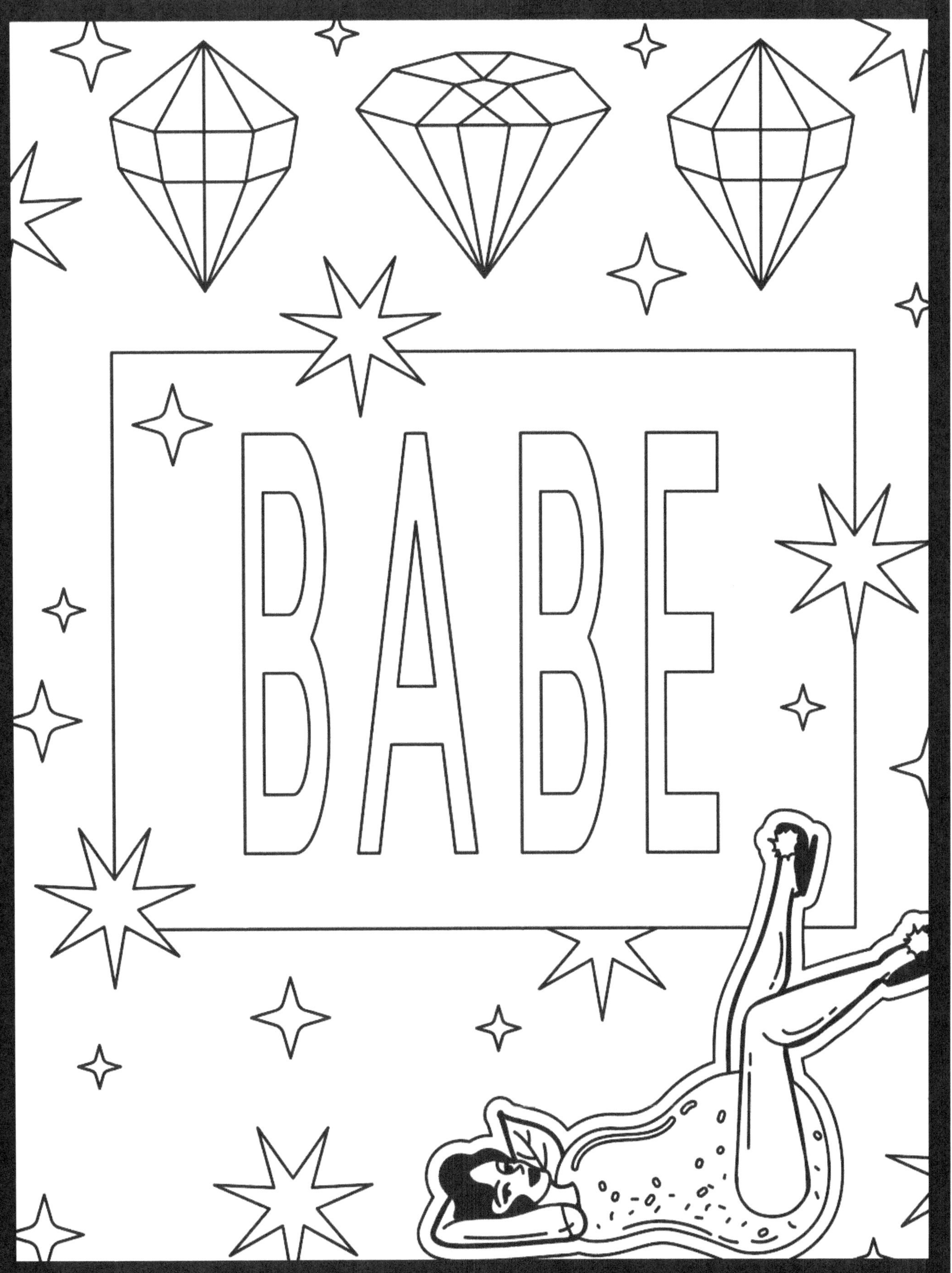

BABE

PEAR SHAPED BABE

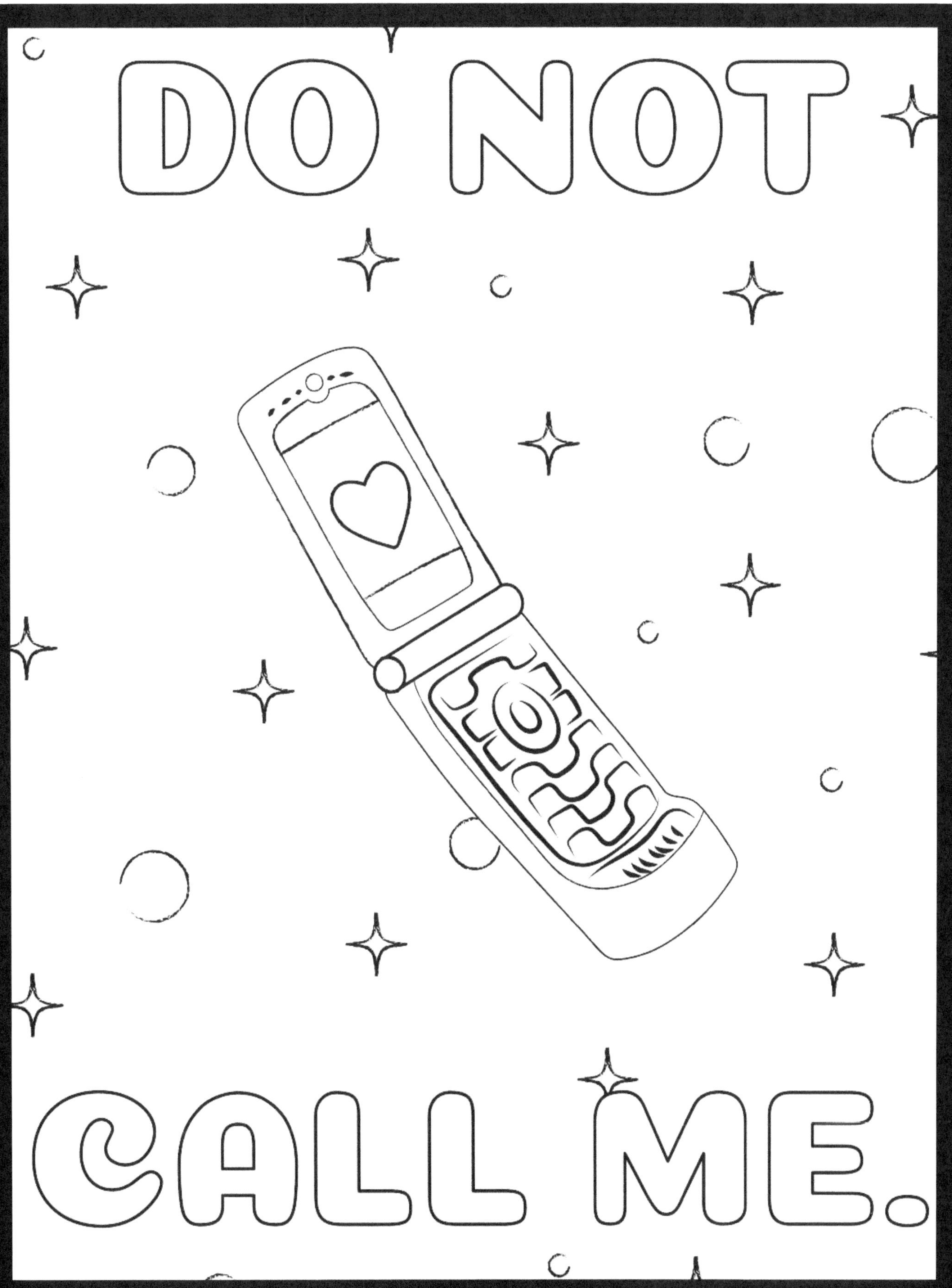
DO NOT
CALL ME.

DO NOT EVER CALL ME.

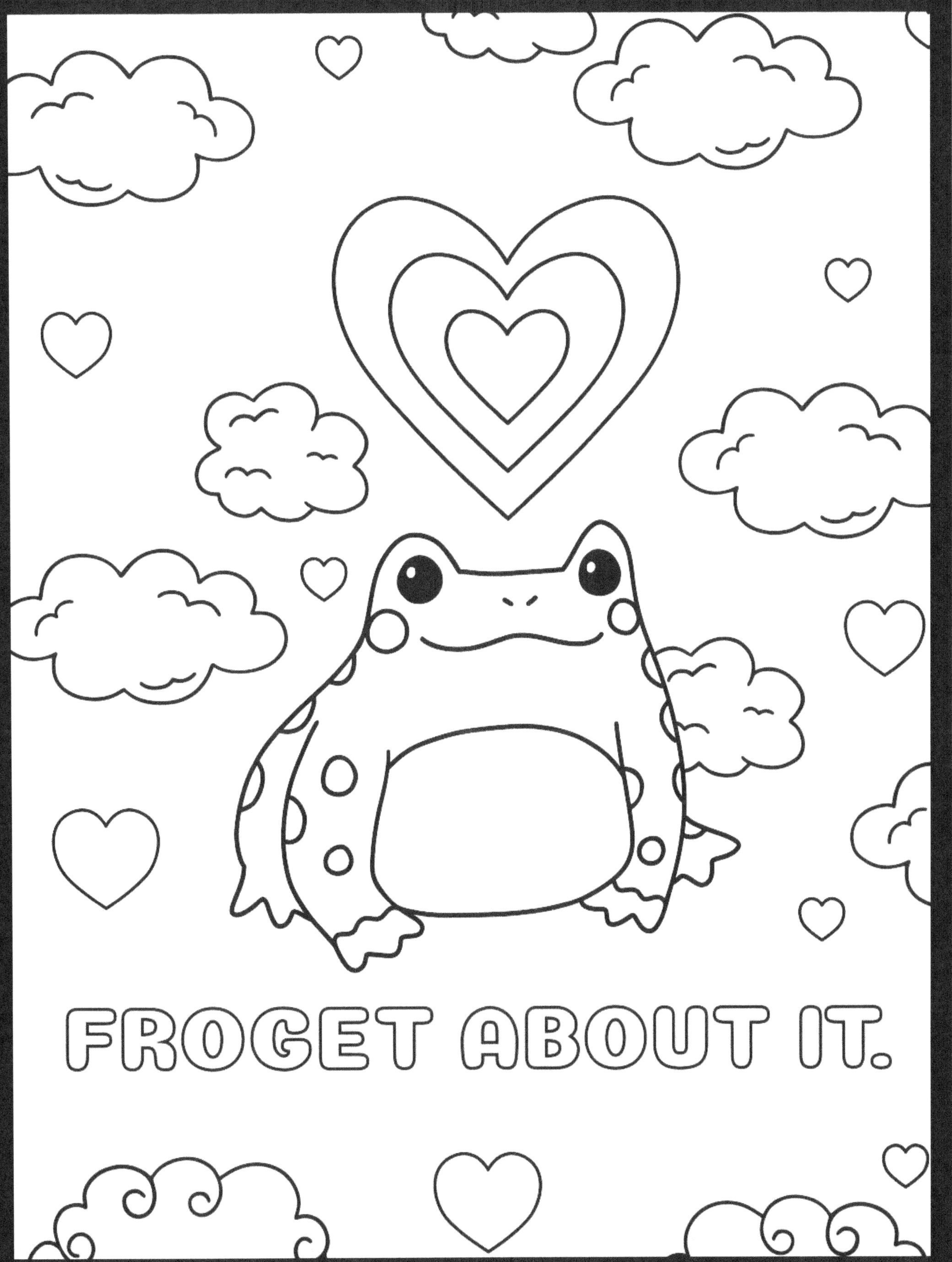
FROGET ABOUT IT.

FROGET ABOUT IT

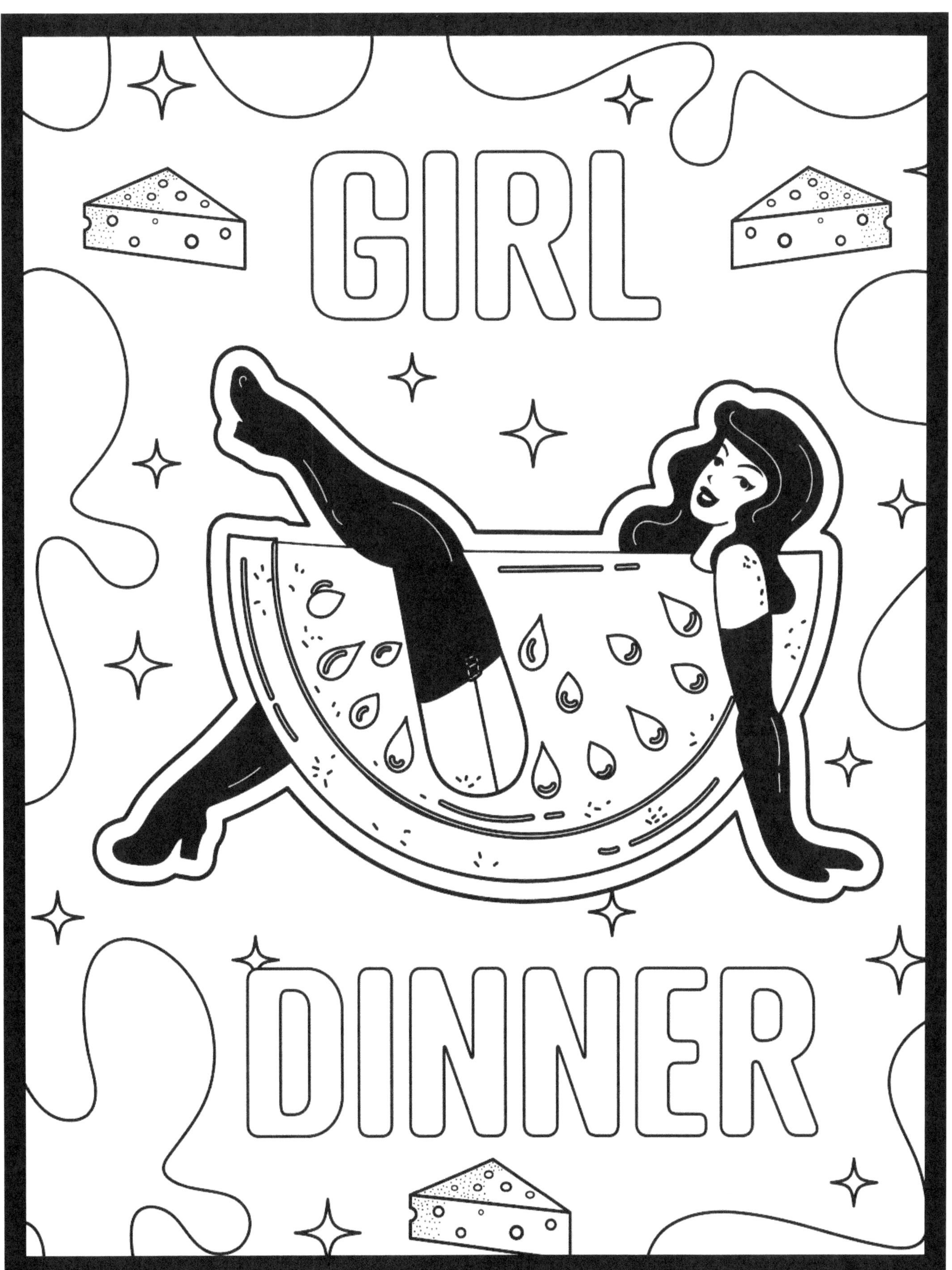
GIRL
DINNER

GIRL DINNER GIRL DINNER GIRL DINNER

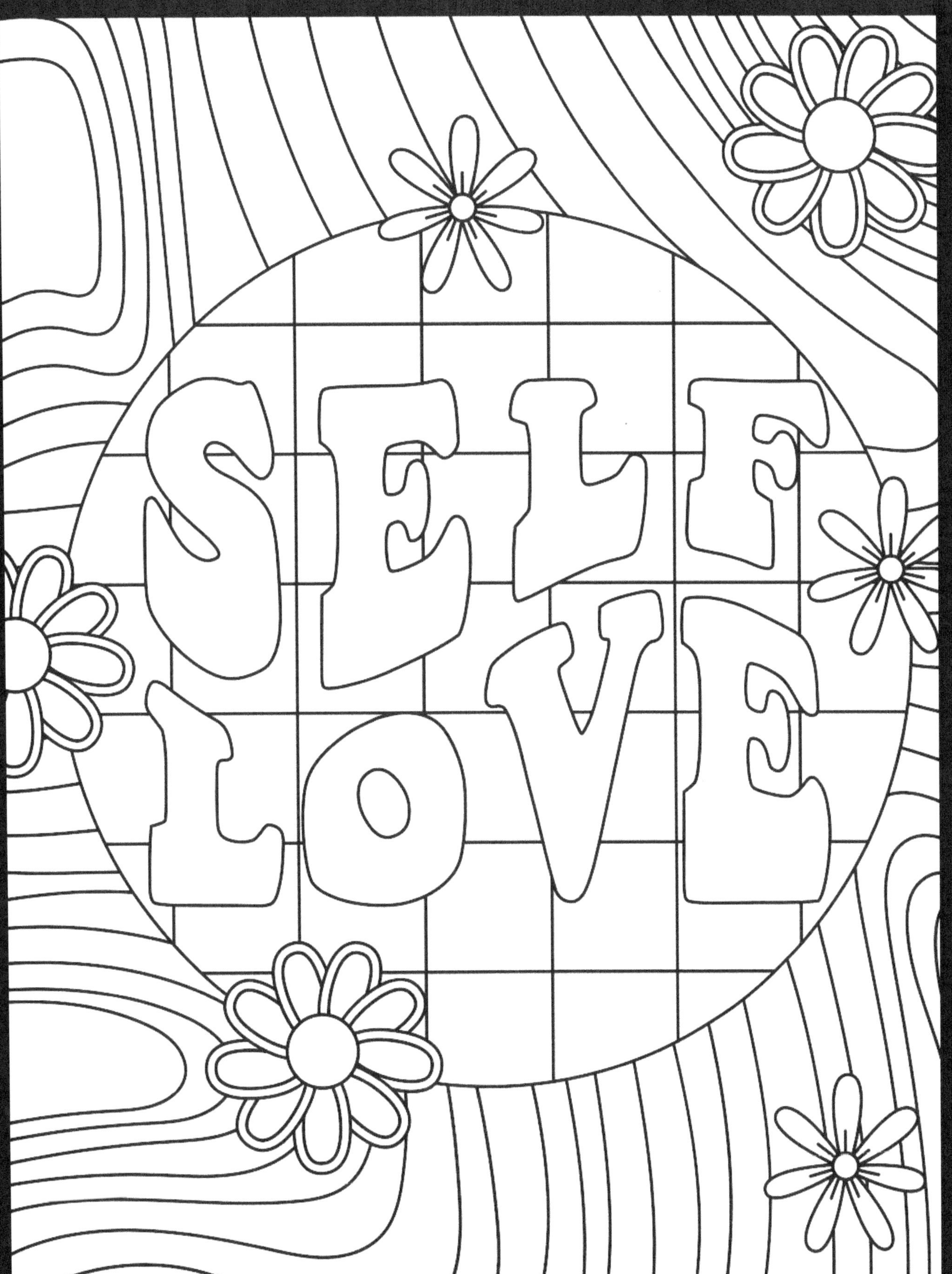
SELF
LOVE

WORTHY

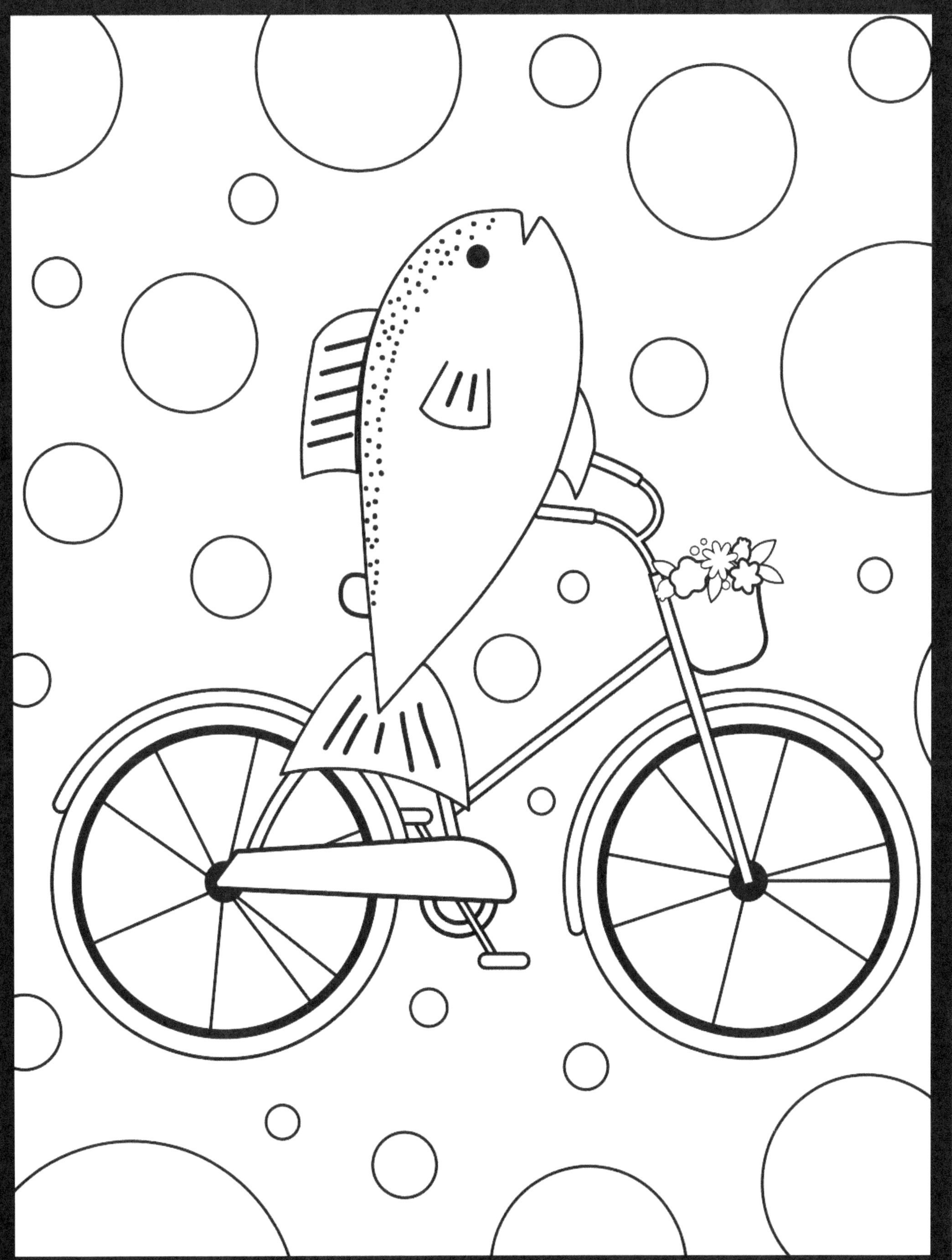

FISH DON'T NEED BIKES

FEMINISM IS FOR EVERYONE!

IT SURE IS

IT SURE IS

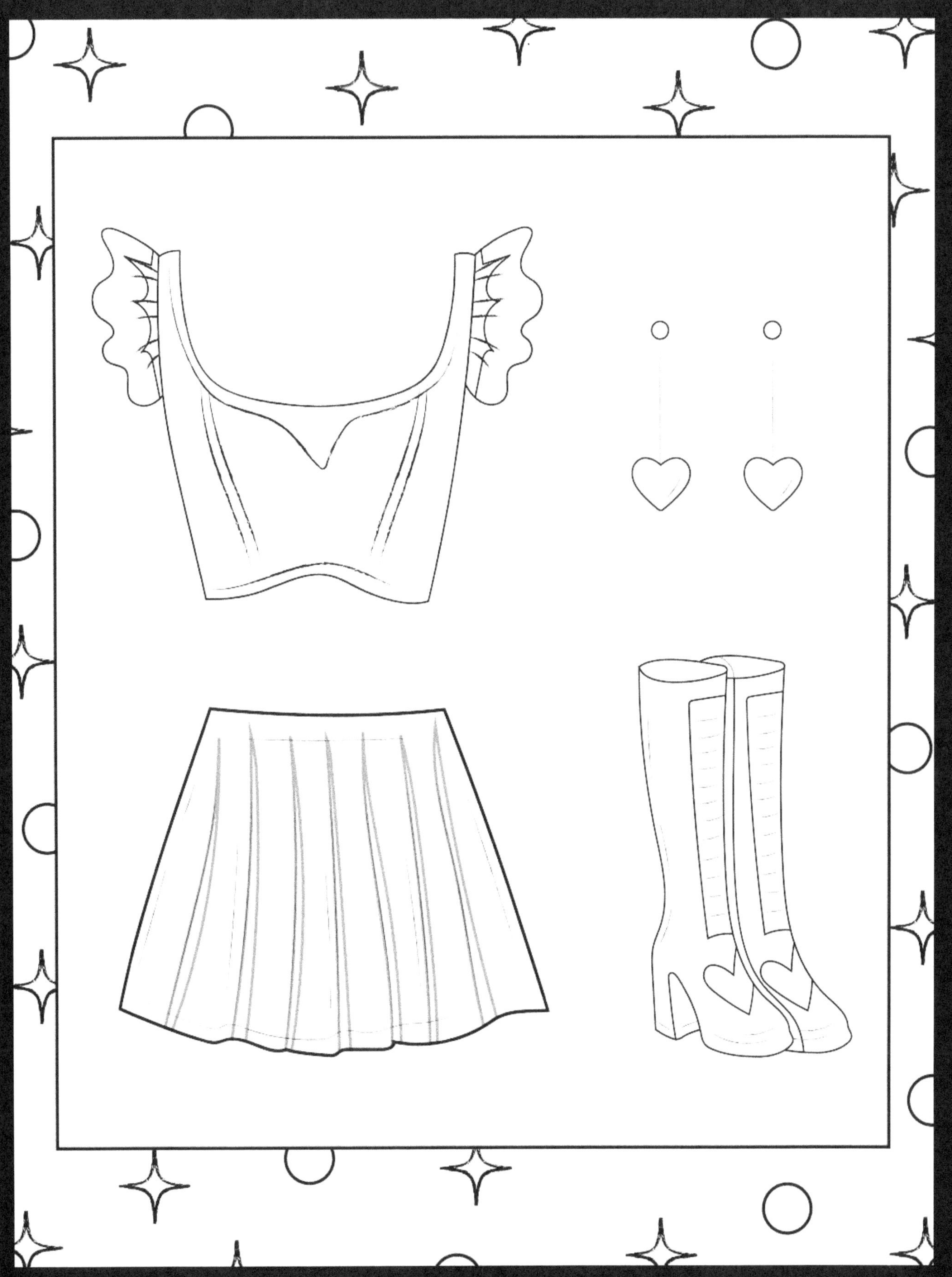

FEELING LIKE DOLLY

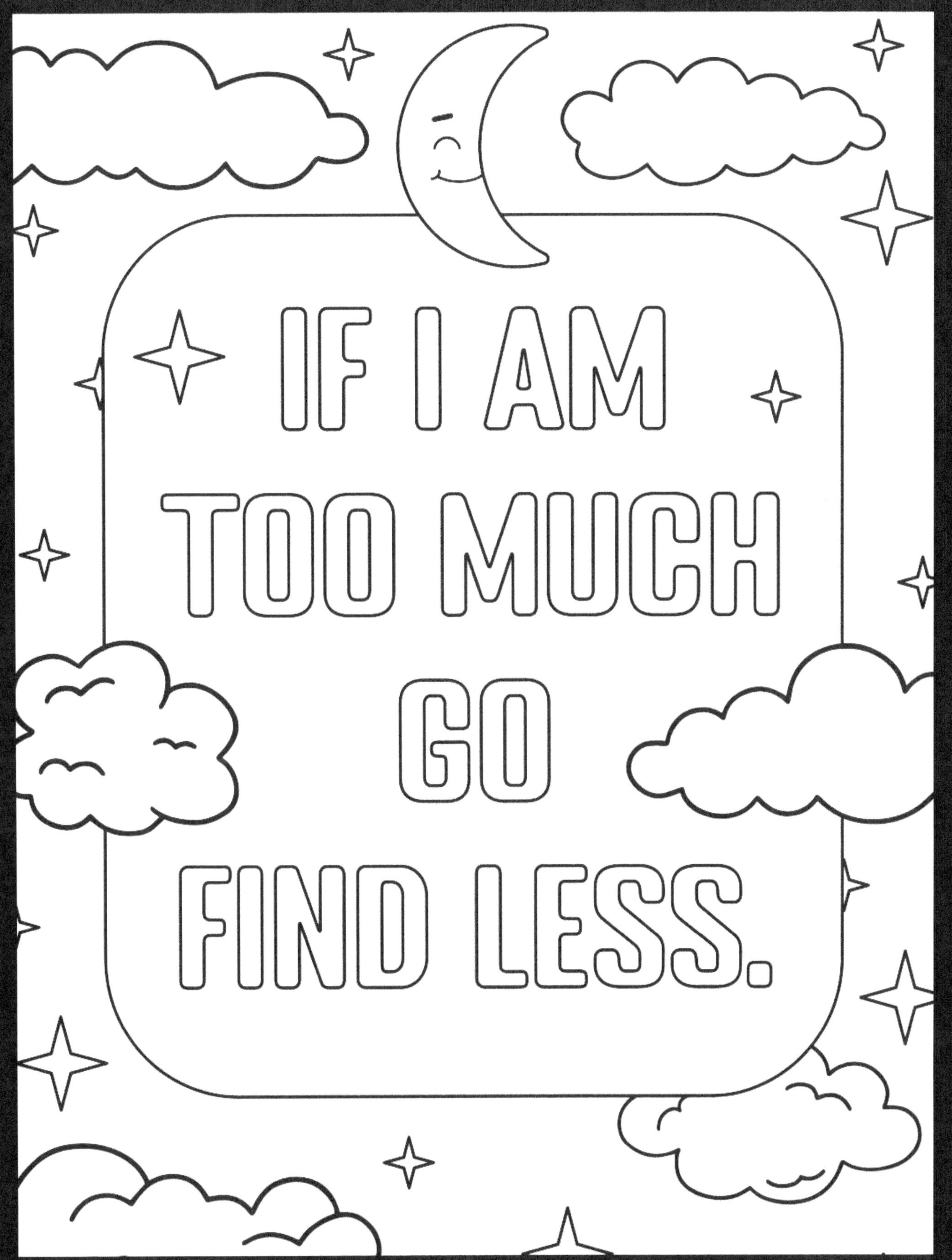
IF I AM TOO MUCH GO FIND LESS.

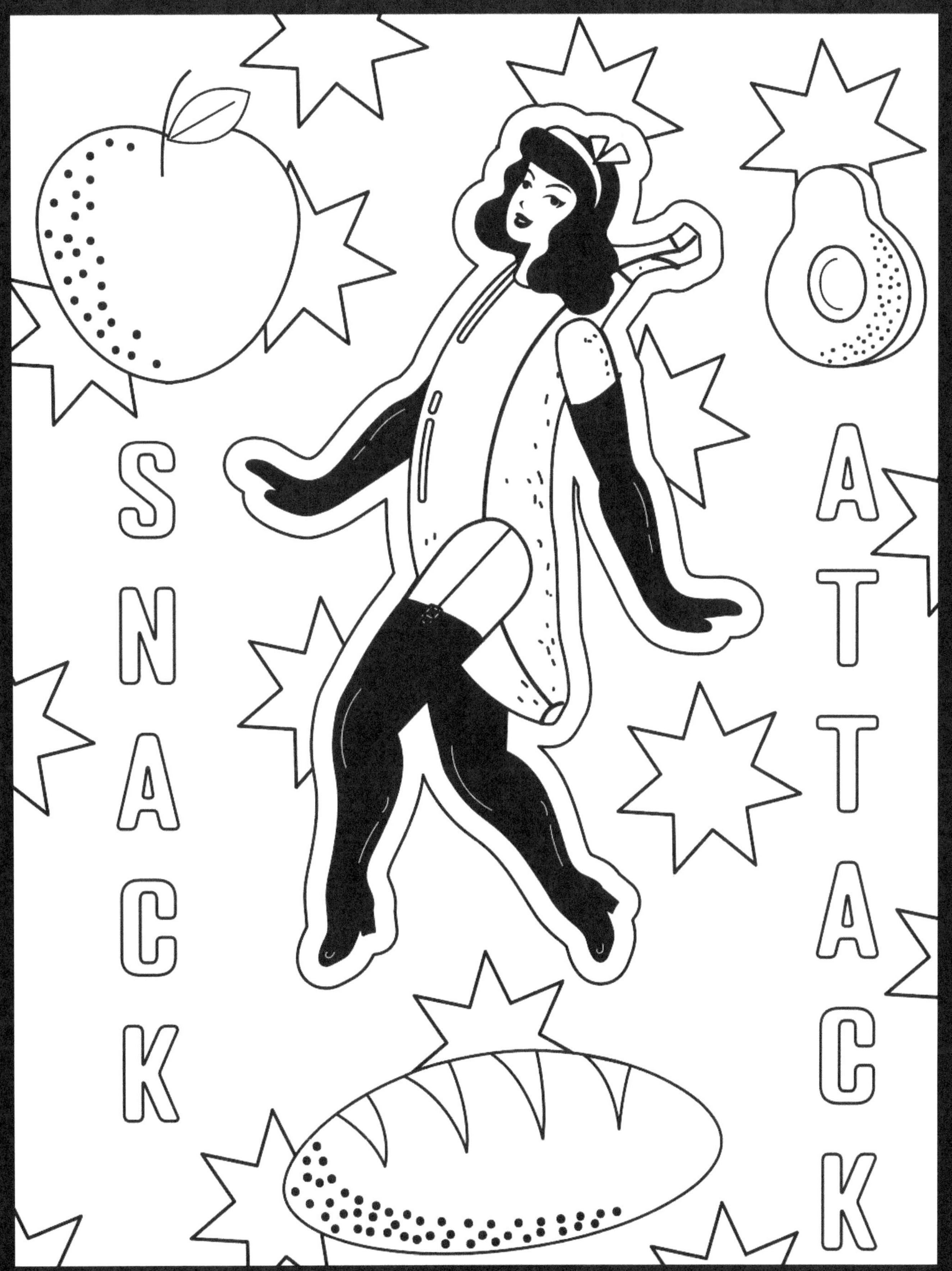

SNACK
ATTACK

SNACK ATTACK

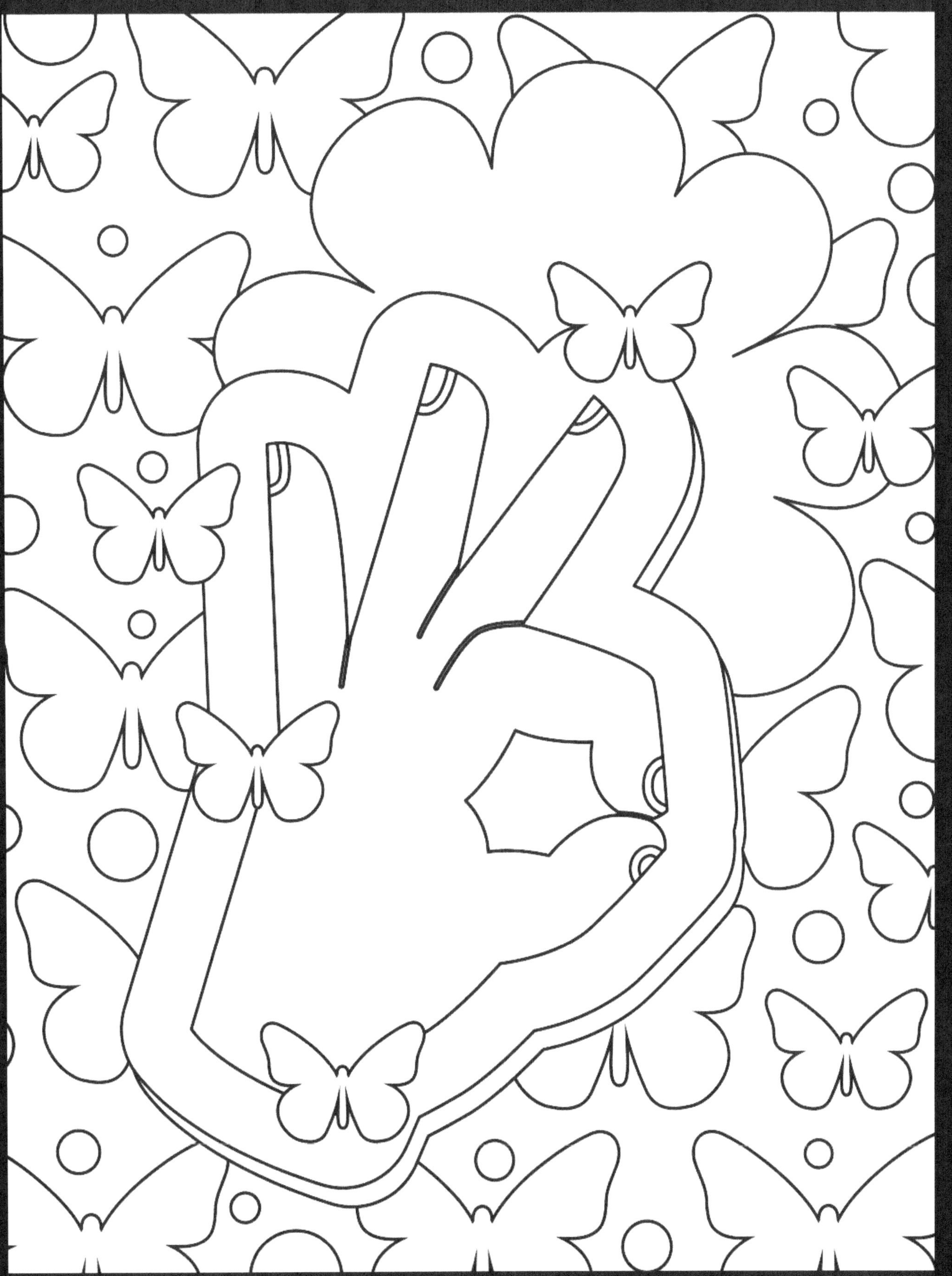

OKAY

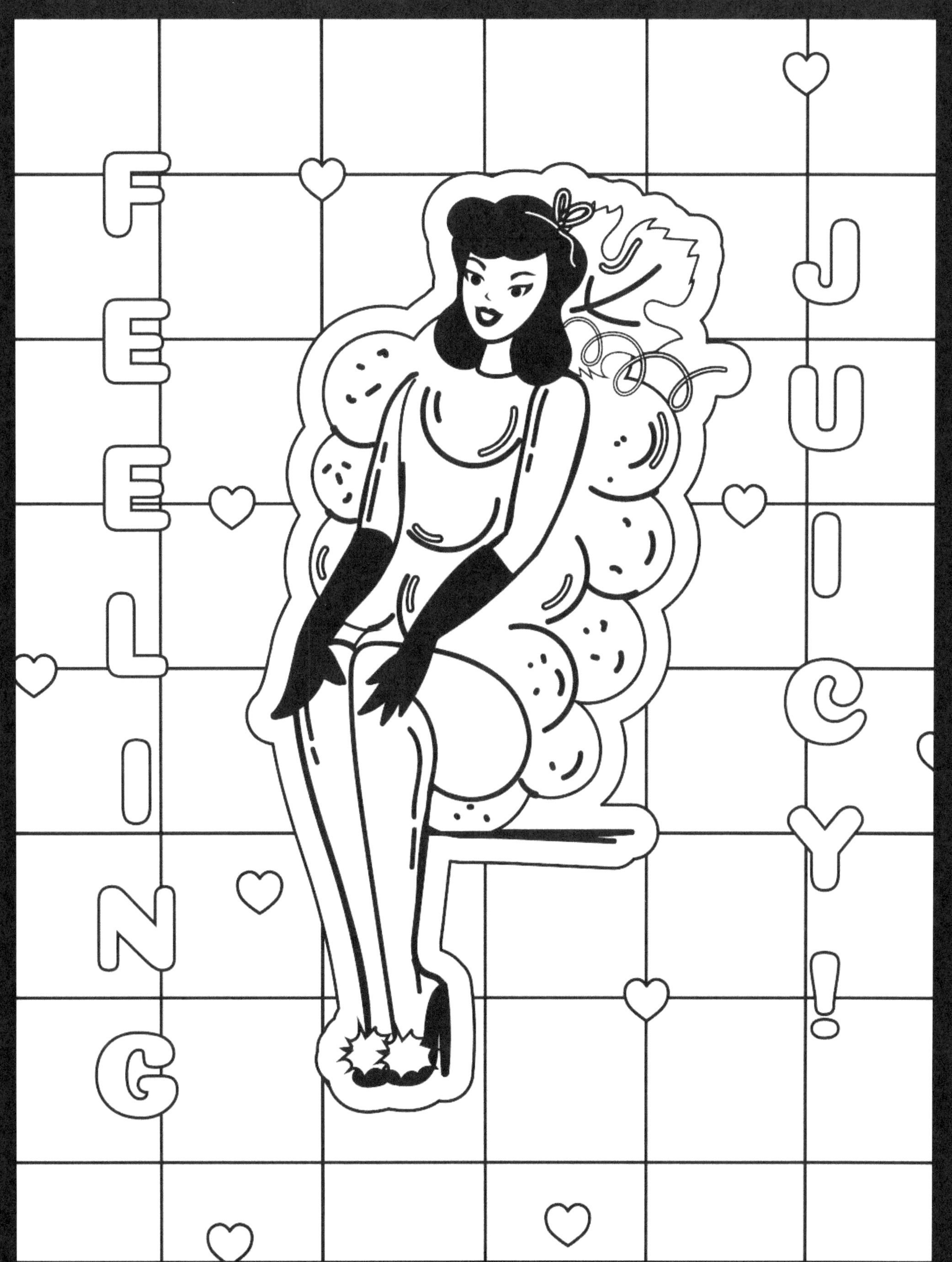
FEELING
JUICY!

FEELING JUICY

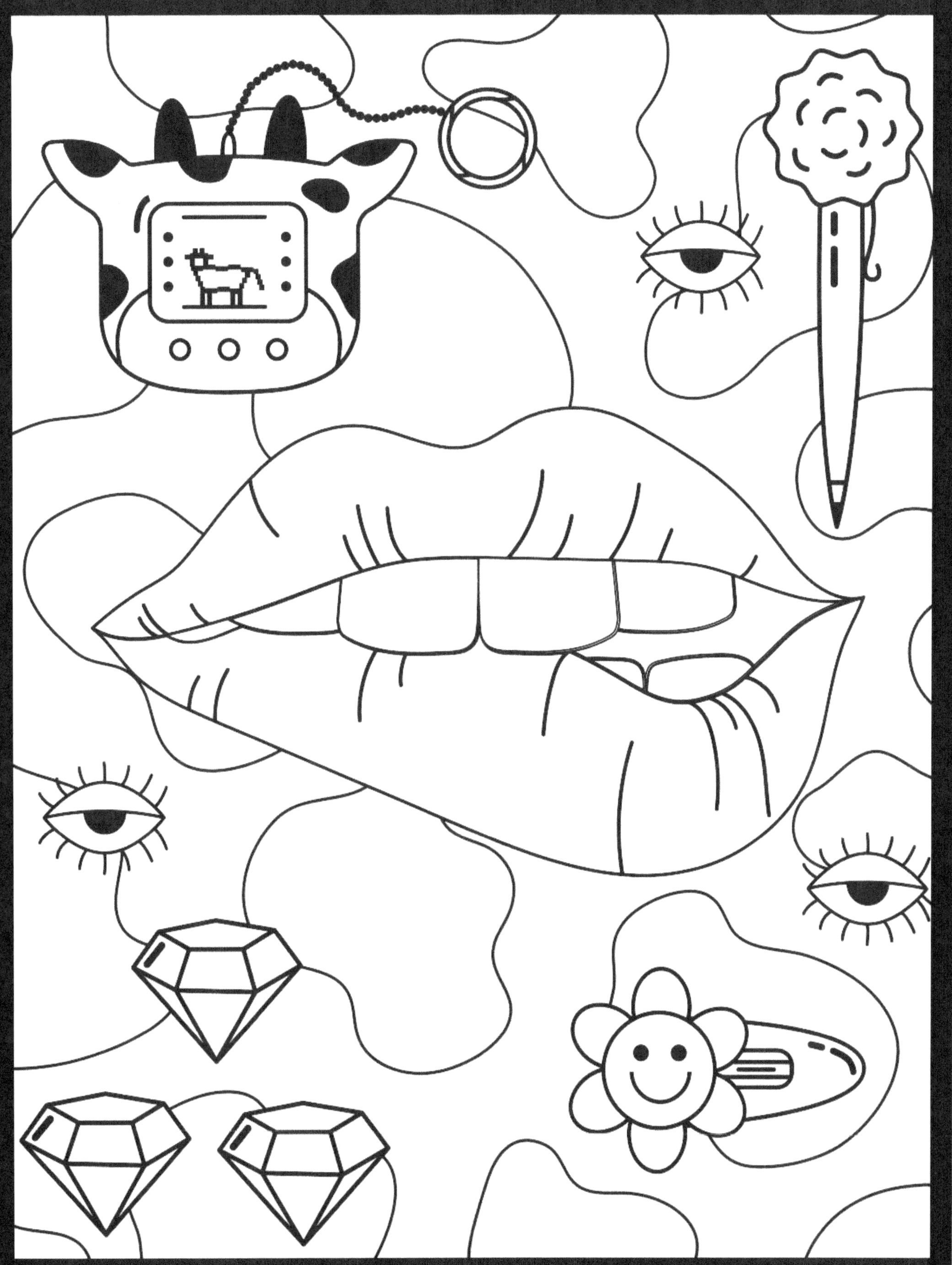

GIRL STUFF

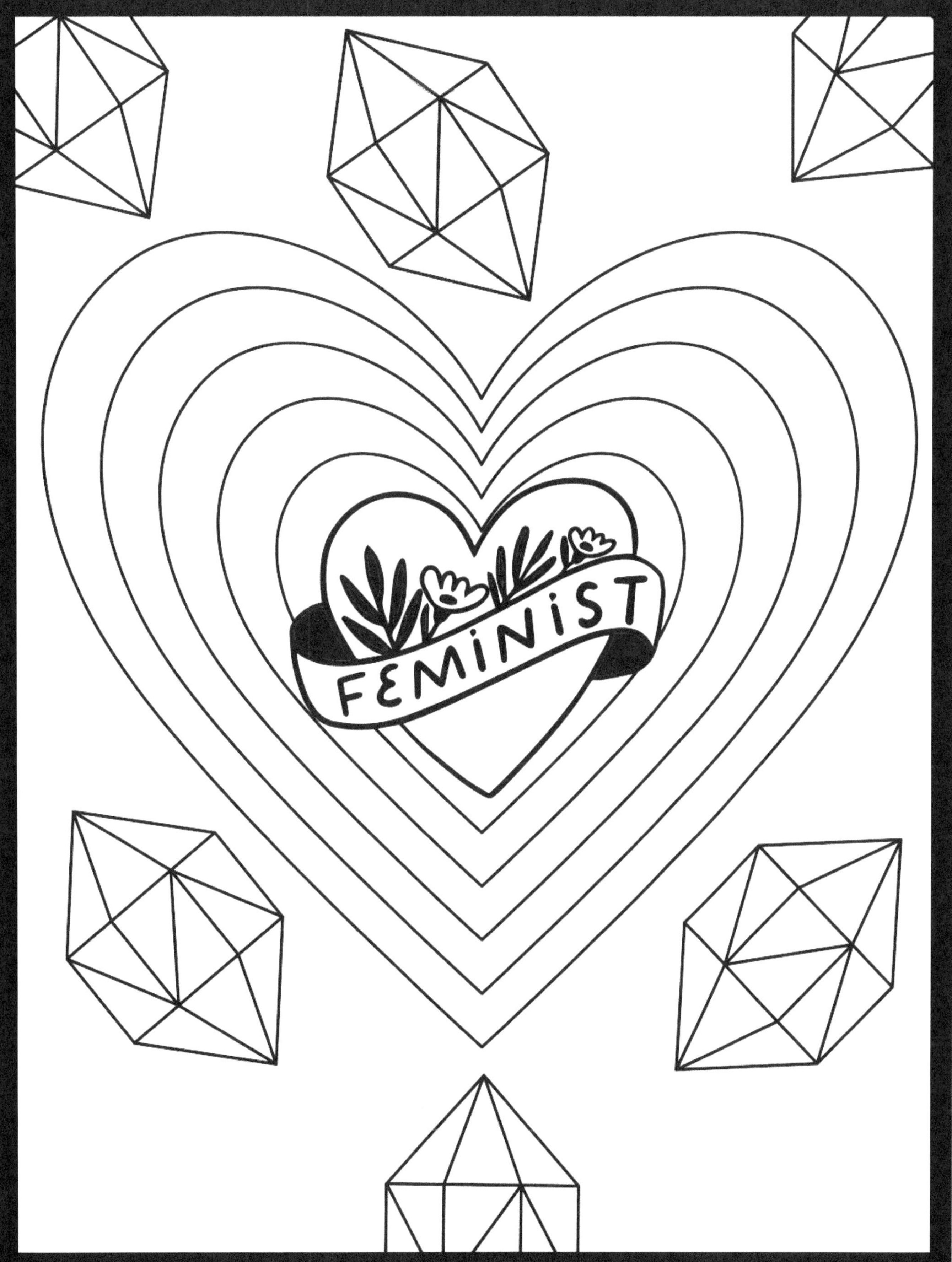

FEMINIST

AT THE HEART OF FEMINISM

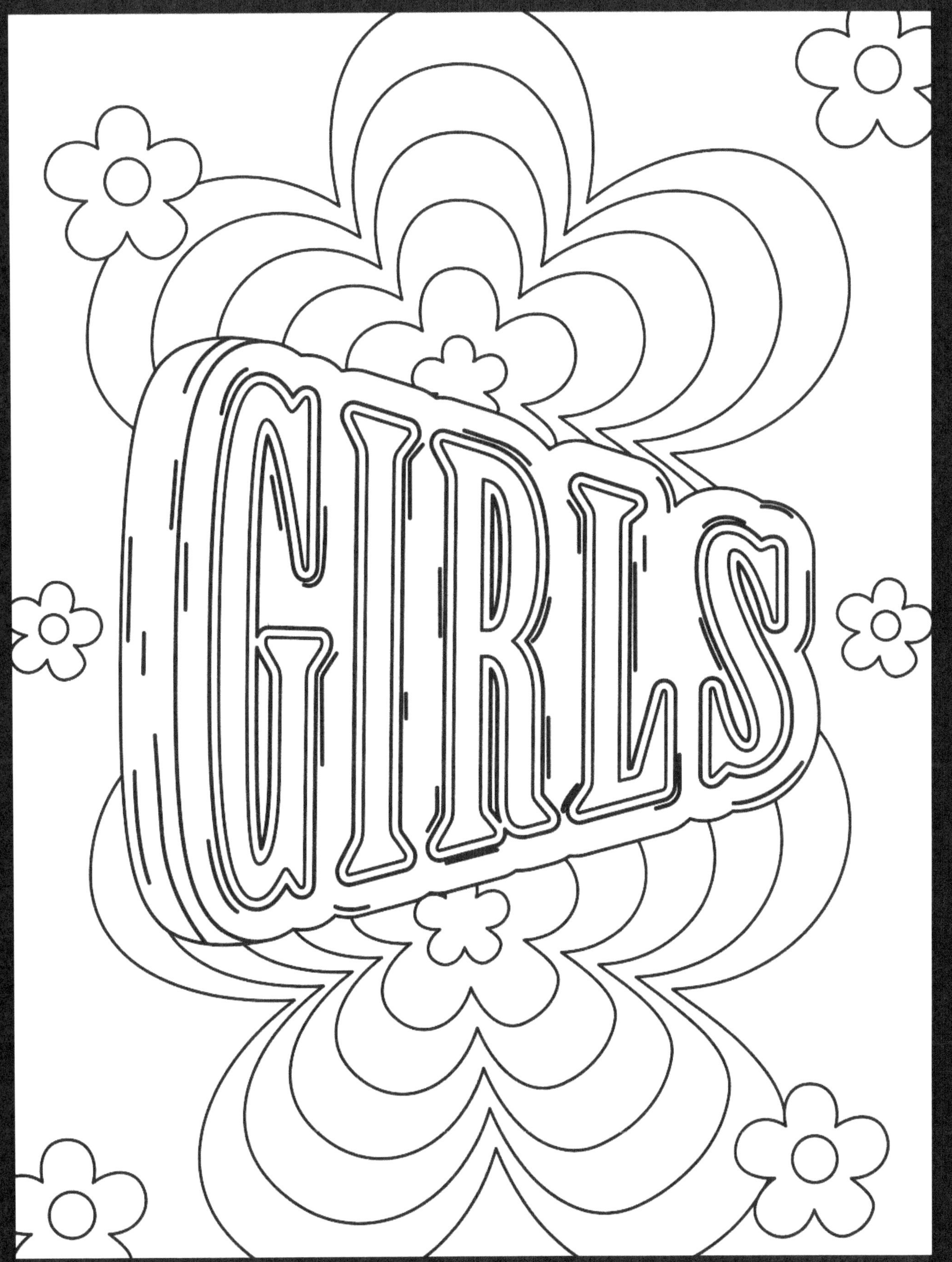
GIRLS

GIRLS RULE

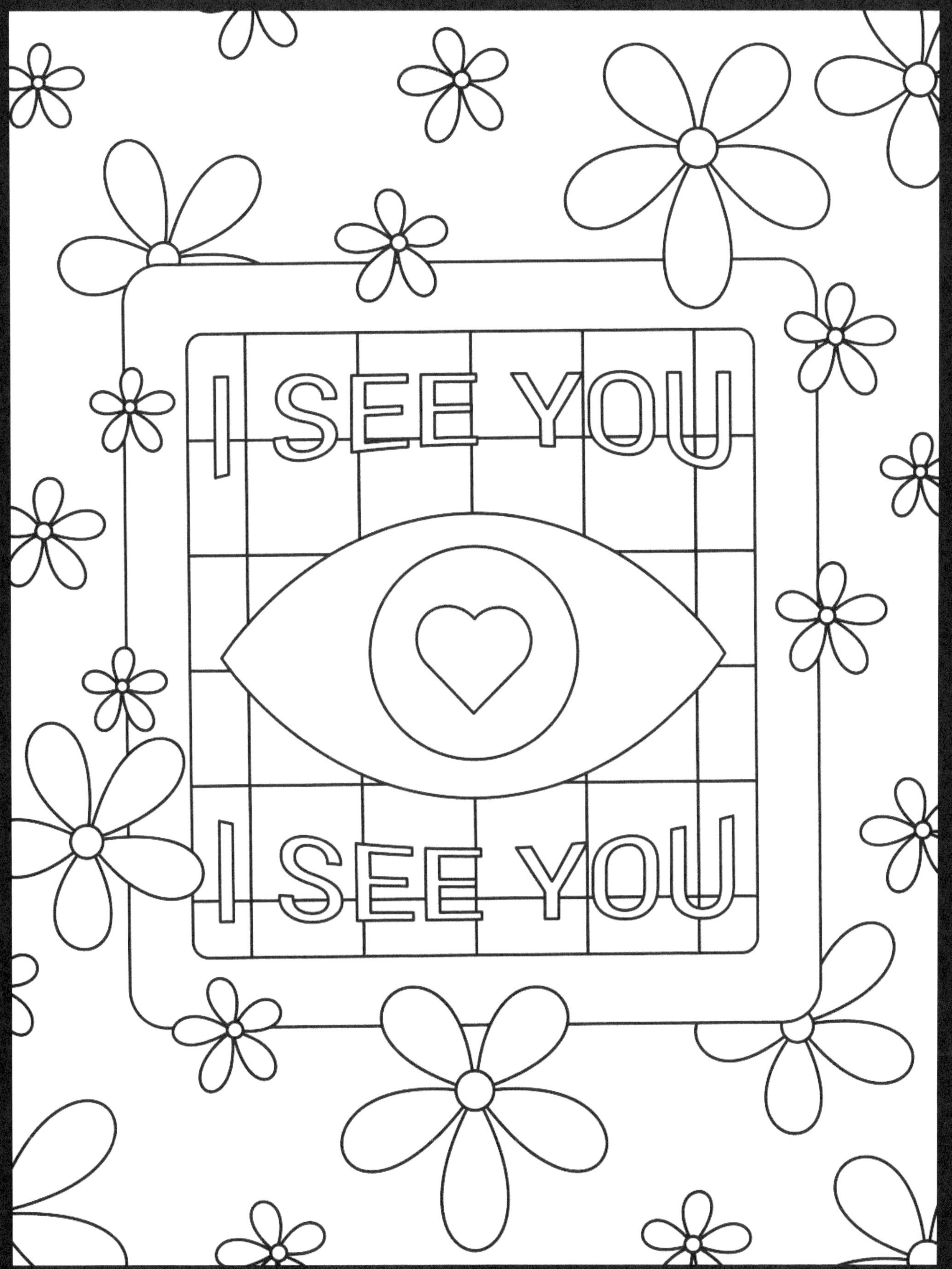

I SEE YOU
I SEE YOU

I SEE YOU

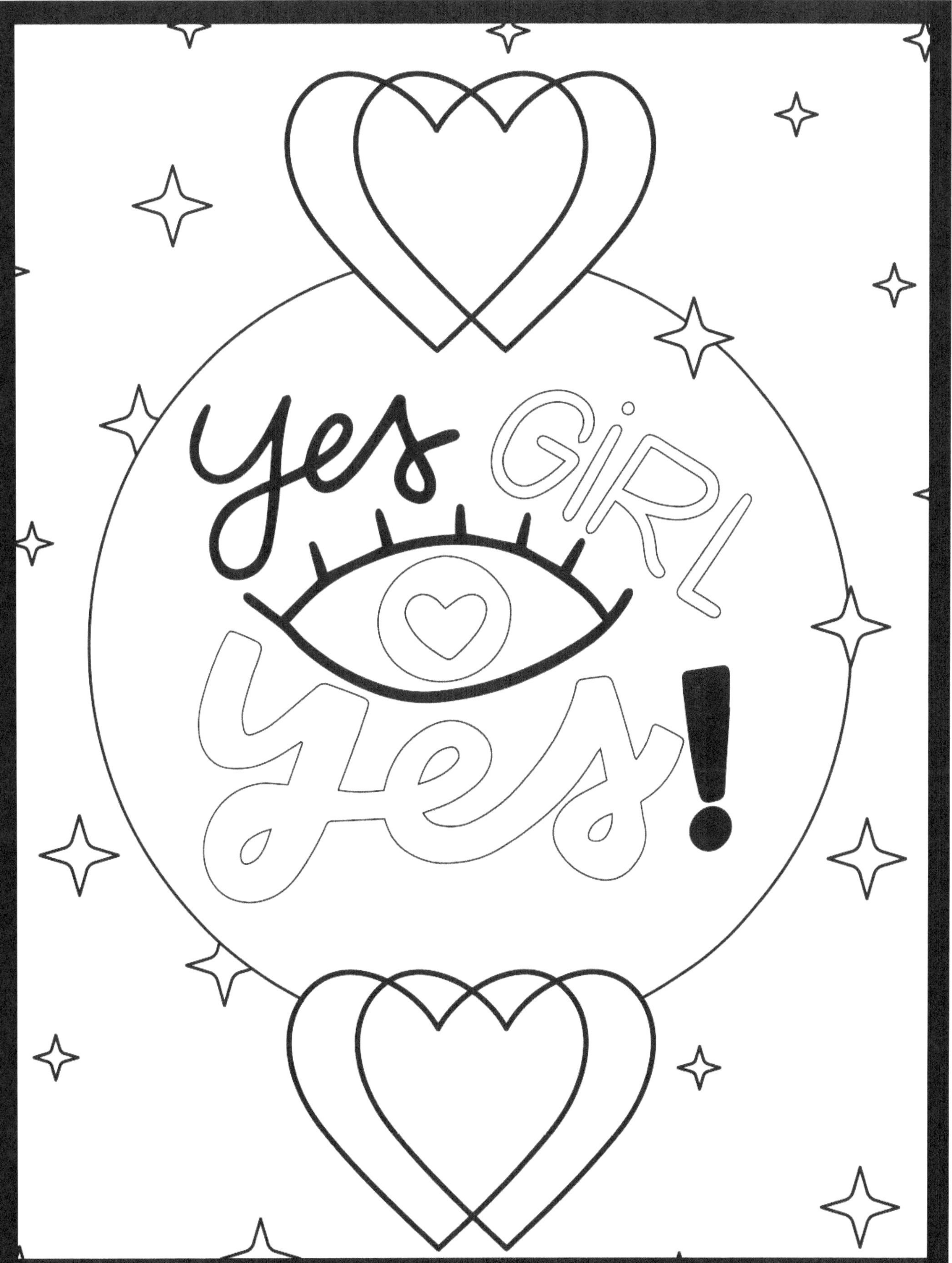

Yes GIRL
Yes!

ROOTING FOR YOU ALWAYS

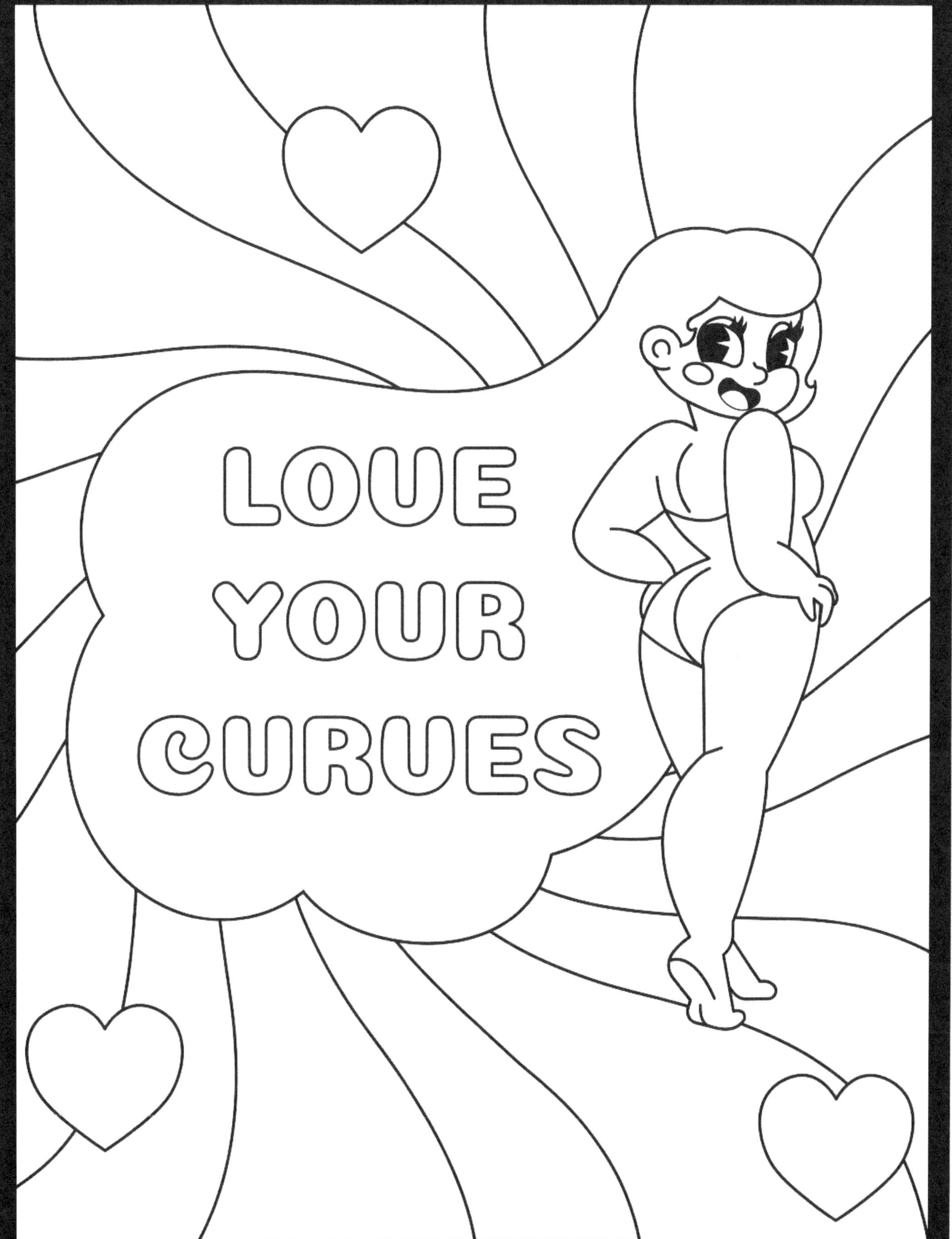
LOUE YOUR CURUES

YOUR CURVES ARE BEAUTIFUL.

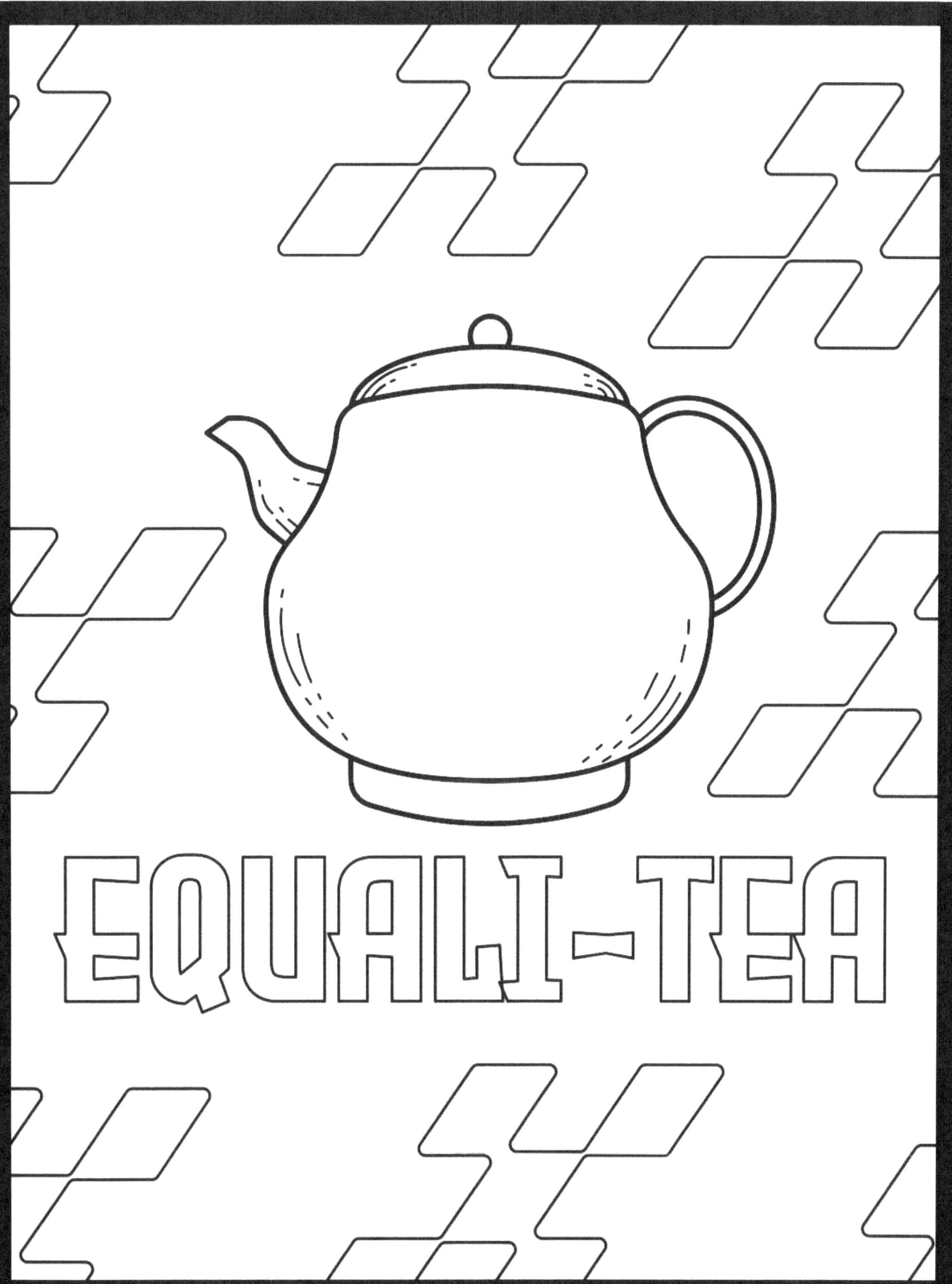

EQUALI-TEA

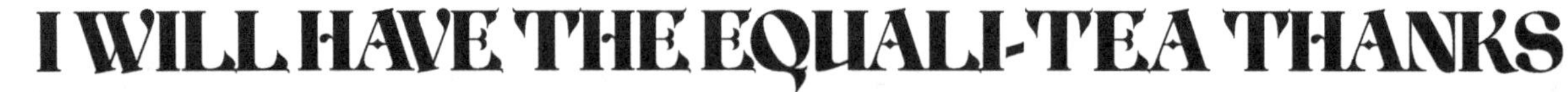

I WILL HAVE THE EQUALI-TEA THANKS

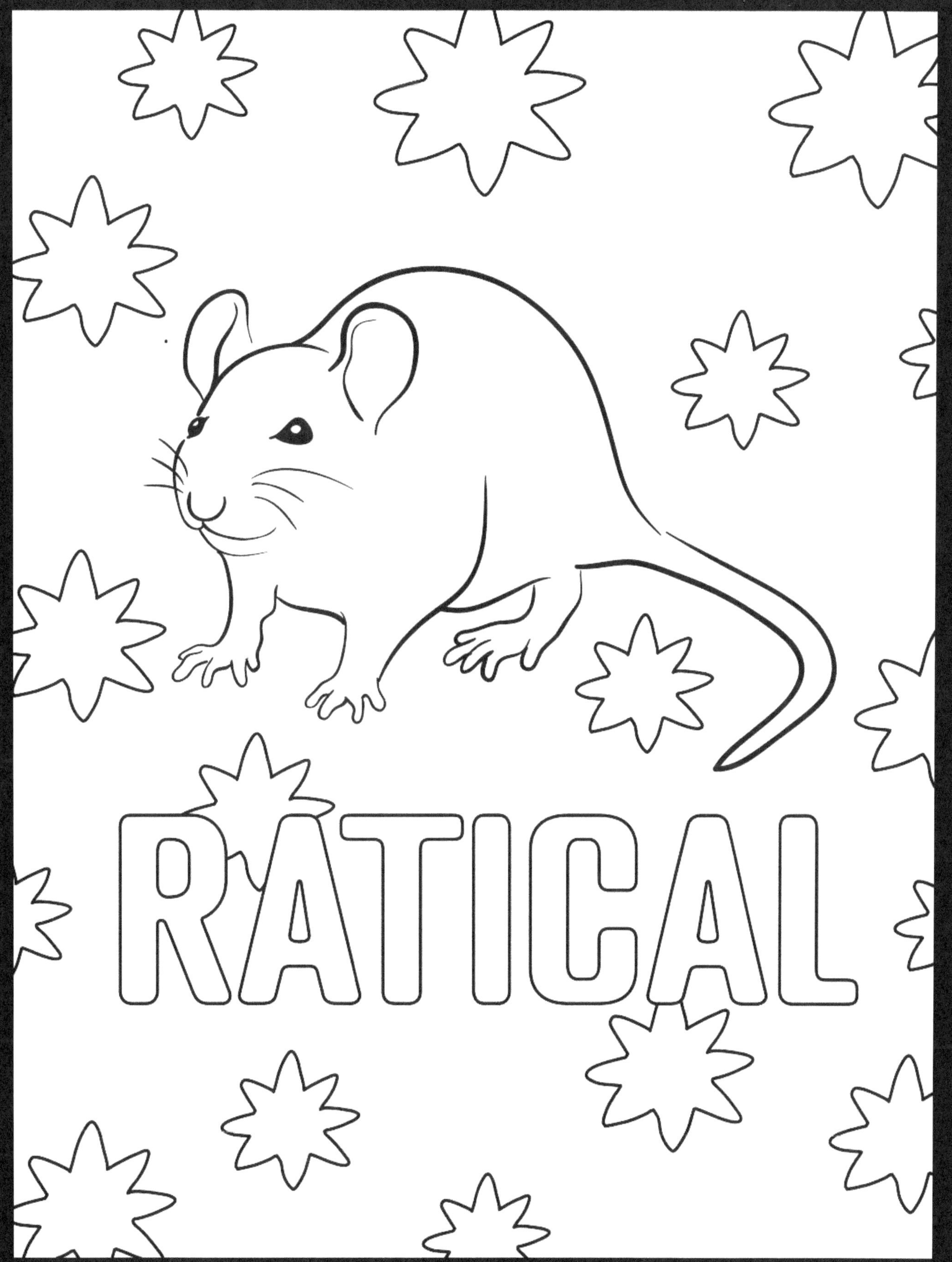
RATICAL

RATICAL FEMINIST

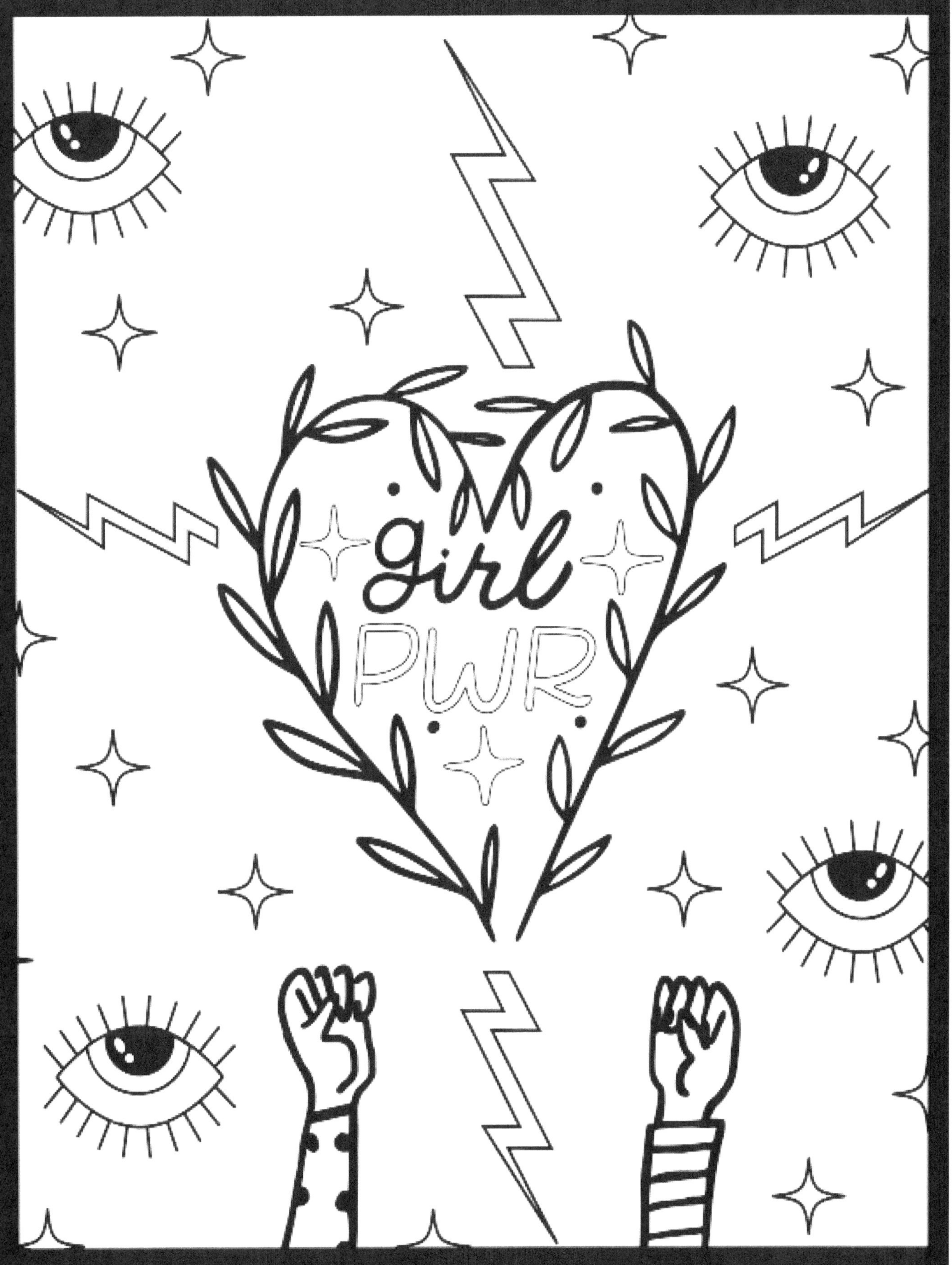
girl
PWR

GIRL POWER

GIRL POWER

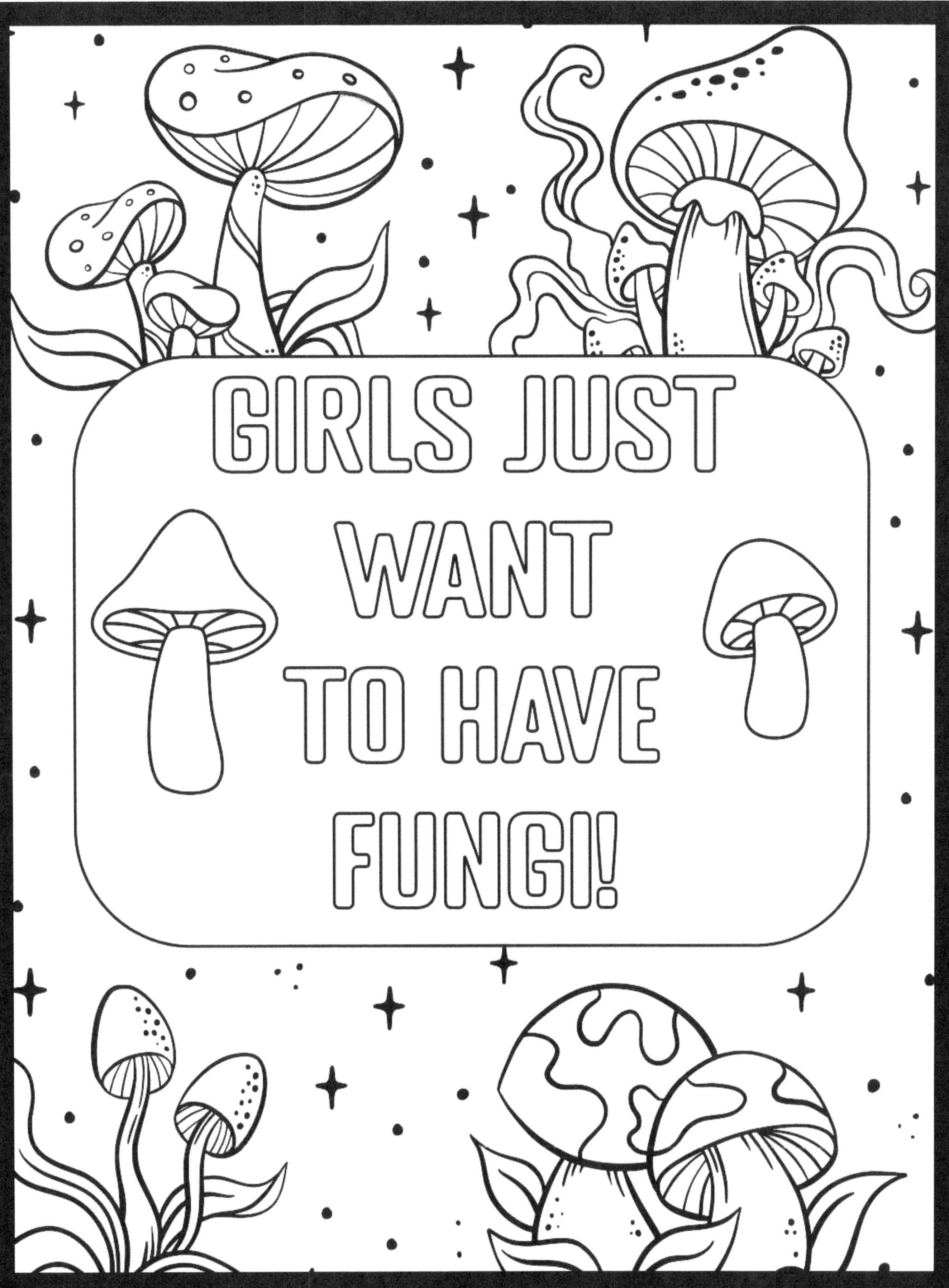

GIRLS JUST
WANT
TO HAVE
FUNGI!

GIRLS JUST WANT TO HAVE FUNGI

COLLECT THEM ALL!

MORE BOOKS FROM

AMANDALE

90S WAVE

DESERT DREAMS

HAUNTED HALLOWEEN

FRESH TO DEATH

METAMORPHOSIS

SPOOKSHOW

TRANSCENDENTAL TAROT

SUPERNATURAL SPLENDORS

SPACE JUNK

AWAKENING

LOVE SPELL

ETHEREAL GARDEN

AS ABOVE SO BELOW

FEELING FABULOUS

BEACH PLEASE

HOLIDAY HAPPENINGS

THE DIVINE FEMINIST

A SPECIAL THANK YOU TO DEIDRE AND BINDER CLIPS. THANK YOU FOR ALL OF YOUR INPUT AND SUPPORT THROUGHOUT THIS BOOK. I COULDN'T HAVE DONE IT WITHOUT YOU.